Please Help Me With My Homework!

I0157253

Homework Strategies for Parents and Caregivers
2nd Edition

Susan Gingras Fitzell, M.Ed.

Cogent Catalyst Publications

Fitzell, Susan Gingras
    Please Help Me With My Homework! Strategies for Parents and Caregivers 85 pp.
ISBN 978-1-932995-12-1

At the time of publication, the information cited within is the most current available and/or the original source material. The author and publisher do not provide any guarantee or warranty regarding the information provided by any sources cited here, nor do we take responsibility for any changes to information or Web sites. If you find an error or would like to alert us to a change to any resource cited herein,

If you have questions or would like customized school in-service or ongoing consultation, contact:
Susan Gingras Fitzell
PO Box 6182
Manchester, NH 03108-6182
Phone: 603-625-6087 or 210-473-2863
Email: SFitzell@SusanFitzell.com
Main Website: http://www.SusanFitzell.com
Interactive Blog & Teacher Resource: http://www.HighTestScores.org
Facebook: http://www.facebook.com/SusanFitzellfb
YouTube: http://www.youtube.com/susanfitzell
Twitter: http://twitter.com/susanfitzell

Other selected titles by Susan Gingras Fitzell, M.Ed.

Special Needs in the General Classroom: Strategies to Make it Work
Free the Children: Conflict Education for Strong Peaceful Minds
Transforming Anger to Personal Power: An Anger Management Curriculum Guide for Grades 6 through 12

DEDICATION

To my son, Ian, who taught me how to teach at home.

Introduction

Recent scientific research has confirmed that we all have different learning preferences and that we all learn best using different strategies. Brain research has shown that regardless of learning style, we all process information in specific ways. This book provides the reader with simple, proven tools to help children increase their academic performance and make the homework experience more rewarding and productive.

With researched examples and processes that have proven to be successful in the classroom, this book offers useful tools that will help your child succeed at any grade level.

For the sake of reading ease, I may refer to "him," "her," "your child," "youth" or "student" randomly. I realize that you, the reader, might be working with a brother, sister, foster child, neighbor, grandchild, your own child, etc. Some of you may even be working with college-level students or adult learners. I hope that the way I have chosen to refer to the "person being helped with homework" respects all possible relationships.

Thank you for purchasing this book. I would love to have your feedback on the strategies that have worked for you or on ways to make this book even better. I look forward to hearing from you.

Susan Fitzell

How the Brain Learns

How We Learn According to Brain Research

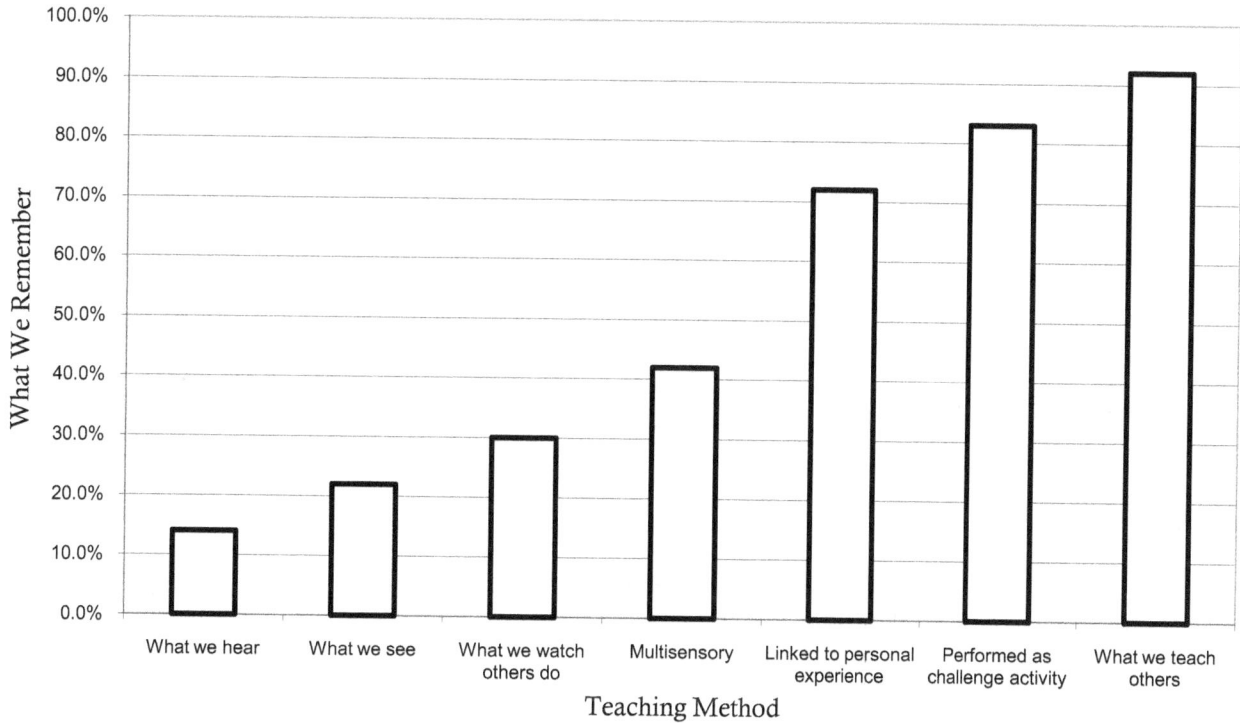

Sources:

Dryden, Gordon. Voss, Jeannette. <u>The Learning Revolution: A Life-Long Learning Program for the World's Finest Computer Your Amazing Brain</u>. Rolling Hills Estates: Jalmar Press, 1994.

Glasser, William. <u>Control Theory in the Classroom</u>. 1st ed. Perennial Library, 1986.

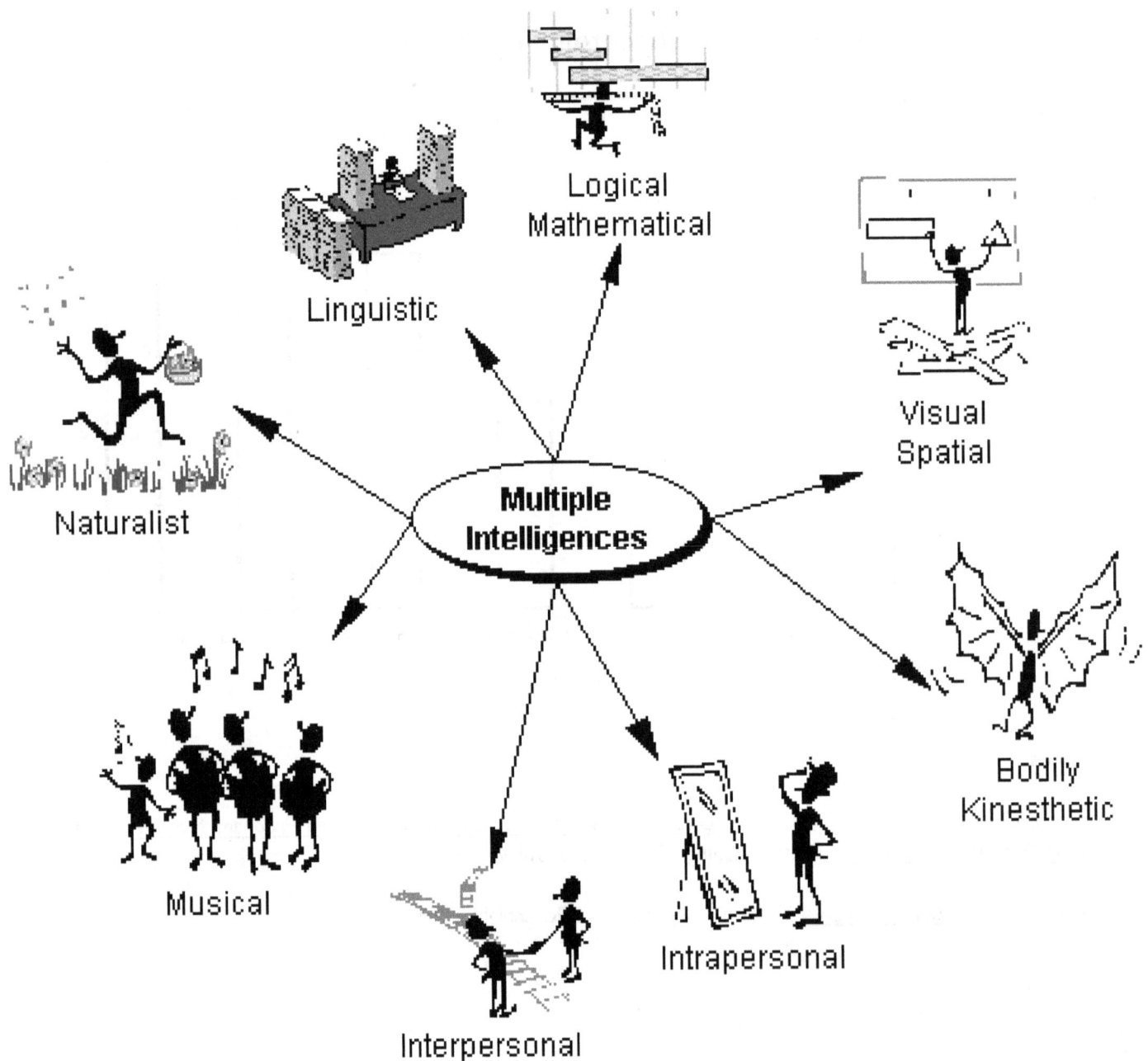

Logical
Mathematical

Linguistic

Visual
Spatial

Naturalist

**Multiple
Intelligences**

Bodily
Kinesthetic

Musical

Intrapersonal

Interpersonal

Assessment Checklist for Multiple Intelligence / Learning Style

Instructions

Read the checklists on the following pages to determine your learning style. Put a checkmark next to the bullets that describe how you learn best. The boxes that have the most checks may indicate the type of learner that you are. This is not a test. It is simply a tool to help you begin thinking about how you might learn best. Use the strategy pages following this assessment for study suggestions. Try them. If one of them works for you, keep doing it! If not, try another one.

Verbal/Linguistic	Logical/Mathematical
<ul><li>Tells tall tales, jokes and stories</li><li>Has a good memory</li><li>Enjoys word games</li><li>Enjoys reading and writing</li><li>Has a good vocabulary for his/her age</li><li>Has good verbal communication</li><li>Enjoys crossword puzzles</li><li>Appreciates nonsense rhymes, puns, tongue twisters, etc.</li><li>Spells words accurately (or if preschool level, spells using sounds that are advanced for his/her age)</li></ul>	<ul><li>Asks questions about how things work</li><li>Enjoys math activities</li><li>Enjoys playing chess, checkers or other strategy games</li><li>Enjoys logic puzzles or brain teasers</li><li>Uses higher-order thinking skills</li><li>Interested in patterns, categories and relationships</li><li>Likes doing and creating experiments</li><li>Does arithmetic problems in his or her head quickly (or if preschool level, math concepts are advanced for his/her age)</li><li>Has a good sense of cause and effect</li></ul>
Bodily/Kinesthetic	**Visual/Spatial**
<ul><li>Excels in one or more sports or physical arts</li><li>Moves, twitches, taps or fidgets while seated for a long time</li><li>Enjoys taking things apart and putting them back together</li><li>Touches new objects</li><li>Enjoys running, jumping or wrestling</li><li>Expresses himself or herself dramatically</li><li>Enjoys modeling clay and finger painting</li><li>Good with his or her hands</li><li>Cleverly mimics other people's gestures or mannerisms</li><li>Reports different physical sensations while thinking or working</li></ul>	<ul><li>Daydreams more than his/her peers</li><li>Enjoys art activities</li><li>Likes visual presentations</li><li>Enjoys puzzles and mazes</li><li>Understands more from pictures than from words while reading</li><li>Doodles on paper</li><li>Loves construction sets: Legos, K'nex, Capsela, etc.</li><li>Often invents things</li><li>Draws things that are advanced for his/her age</li><li>Reads maps, charts and diagrams more easily than text (or if preschool level, enjoys looking at more than just text)</li></ul>

Musical/Rhythmic	Interpersonal
■ Recognizes off-key music ■ Remembers melodies ■ Plays a musical instrument or sings in a choir ■ Speaks or moves rhythmically ■ Taps rhythmically as he or she works ■ Is sensitive to environmental noise ■ Responds favorably to music ■ Sings songs that he or she has learned outside of the classroom ■ Is a discriminating listener ■ Creates his or her own songs and melodies	■ Enjoys socializing with peers ■ Acts as a natural leader ■ Gives advice to friends who have problems ■ Seems to be street-smart ■ Belongs to clubs, committees or other organizations ■ Likes to play games with other kids ■ Has one or more close friends ■ Shows concern for others ■ Perceives and makes distinctions in people's moods, intentions and motivations ■ Good at responding to other people's feelings
Intrapersonal	**Naturalist**
■ Displays a sense of independence or a strong will ■ Has a realistic sense of his or her strengths ■ Has a good sense of self-direction ■ Prefers working alone to working with others, may be shy ■ Learns from his or her failures and successes ■ Is insightful and self-aware ■ Adapts well to his or her environment ■ Is aware of his/her emotions, strengths and limitations ■ Is self-disciplined ■ Marches to the beat of different drummer in his/her style of living and learning	■ Enjoys labeling and identifying things related to nature ■ Sensitive to changes in weather ■ Good at distinguishing among cars, sneakers, jewelry, etc.

Suggestions for Learning According to Multiple Intelligence

We learn through all of the intelligence styles, but we have certain learning preferences that are stronger than others. Choose strategies that support your strongest learning preference.

For Verbal/Linguistic Learners

These learners learn by saying, hearing and seeing words. They can easily memorize names, dates, places and trivia. To help verbal/linguistic learners:

- Use descriptive language
- Have them study by reading, writing, telling stories, playing word games and working with jokes and riddles
- They are good at creating imaginary worlds
- Create crossword puzzles for practice at www.puzzlemaker.com

For Logical/Mathematical Learners

These learners are adept at categorizing, classifying and working with abstract patterns and relationships. They work well with reasoning, numbers, abstractions, logic, problem-solving and moving from the concrete to the abstract.

- Compare and contrast ideas
- Create a timeline
- Classify concepts/objects/materials
- Read or design maps
- Use a Venn diagram to explain...
- Teach using technology

For Bodily/Kinesthetic Learners

The brain's motor cortex, which controls bodily motion, is the key to the intelligence of bodily/kinesthetic learners. These learners process knowledge through bodily sensations and need to touch, move and interact with space.

- Create hands-on projects
- Conduct hands-on experiments
- Create human sculptures to illustrate situations
- Reenact great moments from history
- Make task or puzzle cards for...

For Visual/Spatial Learners

Visual/spatial learners rely on their sense of sight and the ability to visualize an object. They create mental images and learn by drawing, building and designing. Encourage the use of color in their work.

- Make a visual organizer or memory model of the material being learned
- Graph the results of a survey or a course of study
- Create posters or flyers
- Create collages
- Draw maps
- Color-code the process of...

For Musical/Rhythmic Learners	For Interpersonal Learners
Musical/rhythmic learners recognize tonal patterns. For optimal learning, suggest that they hum or sing the information they want to grasp or have them move their bodies while they study. - Create "raps" (key dates, math and poems) or write new lyrics to a song so that it explains… - Identify social issues through lyrics - Analyze different historical periods through their music - Make up sounds for different math operations or processes - Use music to enhance the learning of…	Person-to-person relationships and communication are necessary for interpersonal learners. They study and work best with others. - Analyze the relationships in a story - Review material/concepts/books orally - Discuss/debate controversial issues - Find relationships between objects, cultures and situations - Role-play a conversation with an important historical figure - Solve complex word problems in a group - Peer Tutor the subject being learned
For Intrapersonal Learners	For Naturalist Learners
Almost the exact opposite of interpersonal learners, intrapersonal learners thrive when working alone. Self-paced instruction and individualized projects work best with these students. Suggest that intrapersonal learners keep a daily journal, as their thoughts are directed inward. They have a great degree of self-understanding and they rely deeply on their instincts. - Keep a journal to demonstrate learning - Analyze historical personalities - Imagine being a character in history, a scientist discovering a cure or a mathematician working on a theory and describe or write about what you imagine to demonstrate learning	Naturalist learners observe and understand the organized patterns in the natural world. Provide them with visualization activities and hands-on activities that are based on nature. Bring the outdoors into their learning environment whenever possible. Study in ways that call on the naturalist learner's abilities to measure, map and chart observations of plants and animals. - Sort and classify content in relation to the natural world - Interact with nature through field trips - Encourage learning in natural surroundings - Categorize facts about…

Strategies for Setting Up a Homework Environment

- Provide a comfortable place in which to work without distractions
- If possible, use full-spectrum lighting
- Calm the homework beast with music at 60 beats/minute or less
    - Helps with attention issues and sensory processing
    - Supports organized body movement
    - Assists in actively engaging the learner
    - Increases the brain's alpha and beta waves, which are associated with a quiet, alert state, ready for learning
    - Helps to provide structure for organized thinking, ex. writing reports or papers or doing activities that involve planning

Music suggestions:
- Native American Flute
- Peruvian Mantra
- Mozart for Learning (Caution: Some Classical is too rambunctious. The key is 60 beats per minute or less.)
- Enya
- Typically, music without words (which may be distracting)

You can easily determine the beat of the music using the second hand of your watch or clock.

Paper & Pencil Strategies

- Have children print the information to be memorized
- Put a border around key spelling words, people, places, etc.
- Have children use two colors when working, alternating the color of each fact they are writing in their notes. Color makes facts stand out as unique. If all notes are in one color, nothing stands out as unique and is therefore harder to remember.
  - Highlight
  - Alternate color gel pens, markers, crayons, etc.
- Put a border around key spelling words, people, places, etc. See example below.

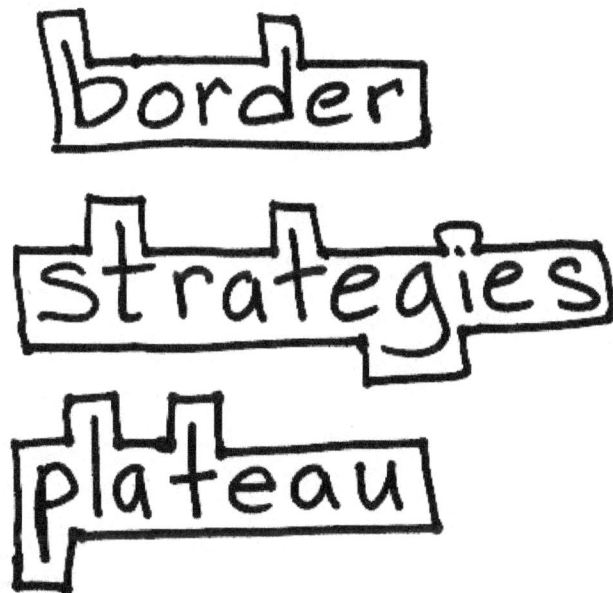

border

strategies

plateau

Mind & Body Connection Strategies

- Use movement to enhance memory
    - Act out vocabulary words
    - Come up with a gesture to represent key people, places or things
    - Use sign language
    - Basketball spelling:
        - If you have a hoop in your driveway, yard or neighborhood, make a game out of spelling a word then shooting a basket. It does not matter what rules you make up. The movement, fun and challenge of the activity are the important part.
        - If you prefer football, soccer or any other sport, use that sport as the foundation. Make your own rules. As long as spelling, etc. is part of the game, it will be effective.
    - Hop & Chunk Spelling:
        - Break a word into spelling "chunks" and hop while spelling each chunk
        Ex. Maneuver
        Man (hop) eu (hop) ver (hop)

Vocabulary Study Strategy

1. Choose a vocabulary word
2. Print it on one side of a "flash" card (use index cards, heavy paper cut into strips, etc.)
3. Put a ⌐border¬ around it
4. Ask your child to tell you what he or she thinks it means, so that it draws from things your child already knows
5. Reinforce the correct definition
6. Print the definition on the other side of the "flash" card
7. Stand and act out a movement for the word while spelling it aloud three times!
8. Repeat the process with the next word on the spelling or vocabulary list.

If your child's teacher requires that he or she write the words three times each in cursive, ask the teacher if your child can write the word two times in cursive and one time printed on a flash card. Explain that you are better able to help your child using flash cards. Some children will not mind writing the words four times each. My children, however, objected to the extra work and even insisted, "But the teacher says I have to do it THIS way!" So, I made a deal with the teacher to have one set of words on flash cards and the teacher then told my child that it was okay.

Brain Gym® - Kinesthetic Strategy

BRAIN GYMNASTICS: A Wakeup Call to the Brain[1]

Brain Gym® is a series of exercises that enables the brain to work at its best. The techniques are a composite of many different sciences predominantly based on neurobiology and have been found to facilitate learning in learning-impaired children. However, the results of using Brain Gym(R) have proven to be highly effective for all learners. There is even evidence that Brain Gym(R) can be used for psychological disorders, as well.

Teachers will find that these exercises enhance student performance, particularly before taking a test, but they also work well before listening to lectures or studying. They may also relieve stress.

How does it work? Carla Hannaford, Ph.D., neurophysiologist, states in "Smart Moves" that our bodies play an important role in all of our learning, which is not an isolated "brain" function. Every nerve and cell is part of a network contributing to our intelligence and our learning capability. She states, "Movement activates the neural wiring throughout the body, making the whole body the instrument of learning." Carla states that "sensation" forms the basis of the concepts from which "thinking" evolves.

The Brain Gym® exercises consider the bi-cameral nature of our brain. The brain has a left and a right hemisphere, each one performing distinct tasks. Often, one side of our brain works more than the other, depending on the tasks we are performing or on how we have developed as human beings. If the two hemispheres are working fully and sharing information across the

---

[1] Adapted from an article by Ruth Trimble (trimble@hawaii.edu)

Much of the factual material for this article is taken from "Smart Moves" by Carla Hannaford, Ph.D. and Dr. Paul Dennison and his EduK(R) literature. Please cite these authors when using this material. Permission to use my data is given, but it constitutes only my opinion and limited practical experience and is not in any way intended to represent the official Brain Gym(R) or EduK(R) view nor to give permission to reproduce the detailed exercises designed by the other authors without citing them.

corpus callosum, then there is a balance of brain function. Without this balance, there is always going to be something that is not understood or remembered. Brain Gym® assists in integrating the two hemispheres, enabling our full capacity for problem-solving or learning.

We are also "electrical" beings and our brain's neurons work through electrical connections. Water has been found to be the best thing we can use to facilitate the thinking process because of its capacity to conduct electricity and assist in cellular function. As Carla Hannaford says, "Water comprises more of the brain (with estimates of 90%) than of any other organ of the body." Thus, a simple drink of water before a test or before going to class can have a profound effect on our brain's readiness to work. Unfortunately, coffee or soda will have the opposite effect, since these will upset the electrolytes in the brain. In all, the exercises that you see here are designed to make us whole-brain learners. Following are some simple but effective ways to awaken the brain and get it working optimally and all at once. Before performing any of the following exercises, DRINK a glass of water.

CROSS CRAWL

This exercise assists the corpus callosum by forcing signals to pass between the two halves of the brain, crossing over the mid-point. The corpus callosum is the thick band of nerve fibers that connects the two hemispheres of the brain and allows them to communicate with each other.

1. You can stand or sit for this. Put the right hand across the body to the left knee as you raise it and then do the same thing with the left hand on the right knee, just as if you were marching.
2. Do this either sitting or standing for about 2 minutes

HOOK-UPS

This works well for nervousness before a test or special event, such as making a speech. Anytime there is nervousness or anxiety, this will help calm you.

1. Sit for this activity and cross the right leg over the left one at the ankles
2. Extend your arms, palms down, and cross your right wrist over the left one. Rotate your arms so that the palms face each other and lace your fingers together.
3. Now rotate your clasped hands downward, turning 270° until they come to rest on the sternum (breastbone) in the center of the chest
4. Stay in this position
5. Touch your tongue to your palate
6. Breathe in through your nose and out through your mouth in slow, deep, belly breaths
7. Keep your ankles and wrists crossed and breathe evenly in this position for a few minutes
8. You will be noticeably calmer after that time

Ruth Trimble states, "My student test scores have gone up because of Brain Gym®. I have children achieving far higher scores than I have seen using the same screening and testing methods for the past six years. The ones who are doing Brain Gym® are accomplishing so much more."

Teaching Each Other

- You and your child will be partners
- Set your timer for 1-2 minutes
- Ask your child to teach you one thing from his/her homework, what he/she learned in class today, etc.
- Set the timer for 1-2 minutes
- You will then re-teach your child one thing from his/her homework, class work, etc. (something different from what he/she taught you. Choose something from his/her study materials.)
- Repeat for one more round

Music as a Strategy

The brain processes and remembers music differently than it processes and remembers spoken words and symbols. Using music to memorize information is a highly effective strategy that is seriously underutilized. Advertisers use music in commercial jingles to promote their products. They do it because the jingles cause us to "remember" their product when shopping. Parents can use this strategy with their children to help them memorize key information needed for tests, quizzes and general knowledge. Children as young as two years old can be taught to remember their name, their address and phone number to music. Singing is a powerful memory tool.

- Link old tunes with new concepts
  - Sing the helping verbs to the tune of "Mary Had a Little Lamb"
  - Pick a popular song and rewrite the lyrics of the song to match the information to be memorized
  - Rap it! Chant it! Clap it!

Here are some examples:

<u>Quadratic equation to the tune of "Pop! Goes the Weasel"</u>
x e-quals neg-a-tive b
plus or minus the squaaaare root
of b squared minus fouuur a c
all over twooo a

<u>Helping verbs to the tune of "Mary Had a Little Lamb"</u>
Is, are, was, were, am, be, been
Have, has, had
Do, did, does
May, might, mu-ust,
Can, will, shall, ...Could, would, should, being

Mind Mapping/Graphic Roadmaps/Visual Organizers

I started using mind mapping after reading *I Can See You Naked: a Fearless Guide to Making Great Presentations* by Ron Hoff (1988). My first presentation was drawn-out like a colorful board game with a route to follow, arrows and picture images of what I was planning to do. I remember thinking how much easier it was to use this technique than index cards with a text script written on them. It also was much less restricting. I did not feel tied to reading the cards. Rather, I looked at the picture and proceeded from memory. It saved me from being bound by a script.

The technique worked so well for me that I started expanding the idea into my teaching efforts. **As I read selections from English texts to my students, I drew the events out on paper in map and graphic format.** I would interject silly ditties and exclamations of passion into the effort to make what I was reading to them stick out in their memory. Given that my students were in their cool teenage years, they would often look at me and exclaim, "You are crazy!" and my pat answer was always, "Yes, I am, but you'll remember this because of it". Moreover, they did.

Children learn and remember mind maps better if they create them out of their own mental images and patterns. See examples below.

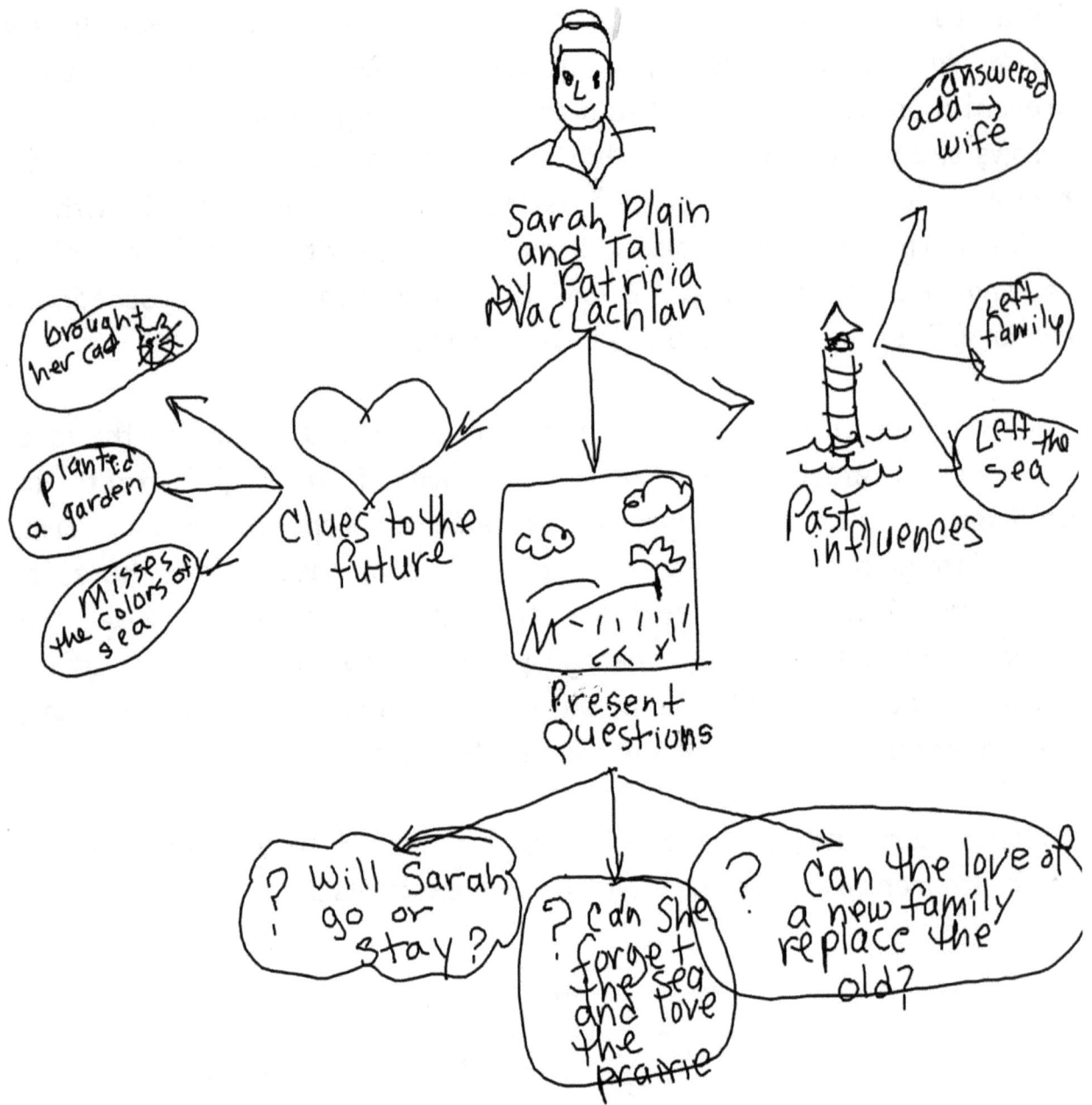

A hand-drawn concept map for "Sarah, Plain and Tall by Patricia MacLachlan."

- **Clues to the future** (heart symbol): brought her cat; planted a garden; misses the colors of sea
- **Present Questions** (picture): ? Will Sarah go or stay? ? Can she forget the sea and love the prairie? ? Can the love of a new family replace the old?
- **Past influences** (lighthouse): answered add → wife; left family; left the sea

When children make spelling errors in this phase of the creative process, note them, but let them go. Correcting children's spelling while they are creating will cause them to clutter their working memory with rules, leaving no "space" for coming up with ideas. So, correct the difference between "add" and "ad" later.

Patterns to Intelligence

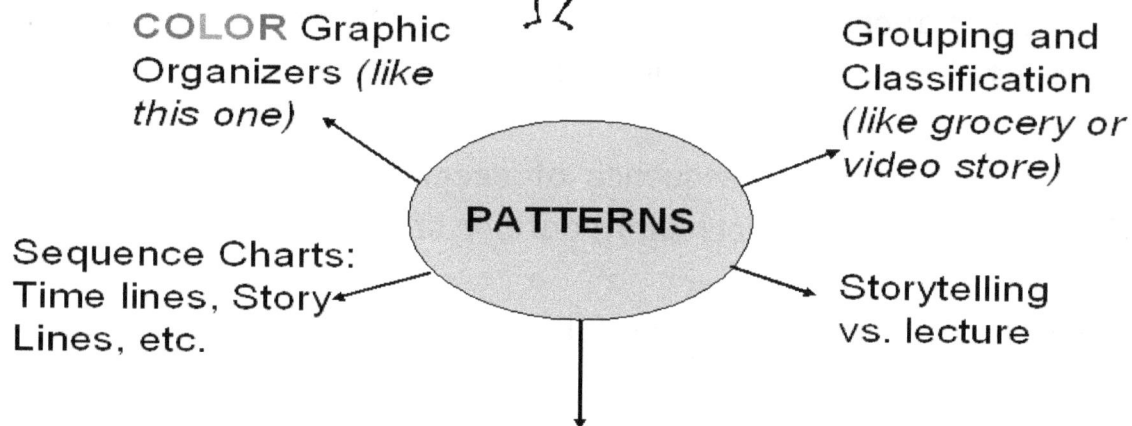

COLOR Graphic Organizers *(like this one)*

Grouping and Classification *(like grocery or video store)*

Sequence Charts: Time lines, Story Lines, etc.

PATTERNS

Storytelling vs. lecture

Ask kids to find patterns: *cause and effect,* problem and solution, intense drama and down time.

Mnemonic Devices [2]

Mnemonic: *(n.)* A device, such as a formula or rhyme, used as an aid in remembering.

Mnemonics, or the science and art of aiding memory, is an ancient concept. Many people rely on mnemonic devices to help remember what they have learned or need to recall, from grocery lists and people's names to kings and queens or the presidents. What works for one person may not work for another. The following five memory devices will help to improve retention of information.

Some examples of mnemonics:
- **I AM A PERSON**: The 4 Oceans (**I**ndian, **A**rctic, **A**tlantic, **P**acific)
- **HOMES**: **H**uron, **O**ntario, **M**ichigan, **E**rie, **S**uperior: the Great Lakes in North America

The best are those made up by the student, as they are more meaningful to him or her.

---

[2] Adapted from the work of Michael DiSpezio, author of *Critical Thinking Puzzles* (Sterling, 1996) for Scientific American Frontiers.

Associations

Developing associations is a familiar strategy used to recall information by connecting it to other, more familiar pieces of information.

For example, memorizing a sequence of seemingly random digits is easy when that number series is your birth date or street address.

Developing associations is also a helpful way to remember new information.

Rhyming

Rhymes and jingles are powerful memory devices. Just think how often you have used the rhyme, "Thirty days has September. . ." to recall the number of days within a month.

To use the Rhyme Technique, all you have to do is make up a rhyme to remember what you want to remember! It is fun! If you are musically inclined, you can even make up whole songs to help you remember long pieces of important information.

Examples:
30 days has September
April, June and November

In 1492, Columbus sailed the ocean blue

In 1903, the Wright brothers flew free
First successful flight

I before E except after C
And when saying "A" as in Neighbor or Weigh
And weird is weird

Chunking

When reciting a telephone or Social Security number, most people tend to speak it in three chunks. For example, the first and second chunks of a phone number consist of three digits and the third chunk contains four digits. Chunking the numbers makes a meaningless series easier to remember. Can you think of other series of numbers that are frequently chunked?

800-566-3712

Chunking is also an excellent strategy for remembering how to spell words. An example of chunking follows:

man EU ver

Other examples:
ALBU QUER QUE
RE NUMER ATION
PENN SYLVAN IA
CZ ECHO SLO VAKIA
LEU KE MIA
FRE NET IC
RECE IVE

Acronyms

An acronym is a word formed from the initial letter or letters of each of the words in a name or organization.

For example:
LASER stands for Light Amplification by Stimulated Emission of Radiation
REM sleep stands for Rapid Eye Movement
NASA stands for National Aeronautical and Space Administration
ZIP code stands for Zone Improvement Plan

You can also make up acronyms to help you remember information. Think of an acronym as a "fun" word or phrase in which each letter stands for the first letter of the item to be recalled.

Acrostics

An acrostic is a memory strategy similar to an acronym, but it takes the first letters of a series of words, lines or verses to form a memorable phrase. Sometimes the phrase is nonsense, which may actually help you remember it!

Here is one: **K**ing **P**hilip **C**ame **O**ver **F**or **G**randma's **S**oup. Each acrostic stands for the biological classification hierarchy (**K**ingdom, **P**hylum, **C**lass, **O**rder, **F**amily, **G**enus and **S**pecies).

Example of mnemonics combined with meaningful pictures that use associations:

Taxonomy

King Philip Came Over For Grandma's Soup.

Kingdom Phylum Class Order Family Genus Species

© AIMHI Ed Programs

Scientific Method

Mnemonic by Chris Donegan

People Really Hate Eating Onion Cake!

Problem
Research
Hypothesis
Experiment
Observation
Conclusion

Use Adding Machine Tape to Remember Sequences

Use **adding machine tape** to create a visual storyline, timeline or sequence to be memorized.

Instructions:

As students read through a textbook or story, they draw pictures of the important information (characters, historical figures, places, events, etc.) on adding machine tape in the same order that the information appears.

For example, when they read about how the Lakota used directions, they draw a picture of it on the tape. Next, the chapter describes the types of information that was recorded, such as position of the sun, the moon, neighboring sites, etc. They will then draw and label that information in the same sequence/order that it is listed or described in the textbook. See below for examples.

Now the students have a "timeline" or "storyline" of the events in the textbook or story in sequential order. This visual memory tool will help them to remember the information in the order that it "happened".

Color and Memory

Simply put, we remember what we see in color better than what we see in black and white. According to Eric Jensen in *Brain-Based Learning* (1996), we remember colors first and content next. Colors affect us on both a physiological and a psychological level.

- Add color to homework paperwork
- Print notes and alternate two colors for each individual point
- Hang colorful posters around the house to reinforce the concepts being learned

According to research, color communicates more effectively than black and white. How much more effectively? Here's what the research says:

- Color visuals increase willingness to read by up to 80 percent[3]
- Using color can increase motivation and participation by up to 80 percent[3]
- Color enhances learning and improves retention by more than 75 percent[4]
- Color accounts for 60 percent of the acceptance or rejection of an object and is a critical factor in the success of any visual experience[5]

The Meaning of Color

- Red - an engaging and emotive color, which can stimulate hunger or excite and disturb the individual
- Yellow - the first color distinguished by the brain
- Blue - Calms a tense person and increases feelings of well-being
- Green - A calming color, like blue
- Brown - promotes a sense of security and relaxation and reduces fatigue

---

[3] The Persuasive Properties of Color; Ronald E. Green; Marketing Communications, October 1984.
[4] Loyola University School of Business, Chicago, IL., as reported in Hewlett-Packard's Advisor, June 1999.
[5] The Power of Color; Dr. Morton Walker; Avery Publishing Group; 1991.

The Fitz-spell Method of Studying Spelling Words

Option 1:

Use phonics rules to determine which letters should be in a **highlight color**.

These cards were actually made using color markers. All of the pictures used in this handbook were originally done in color.

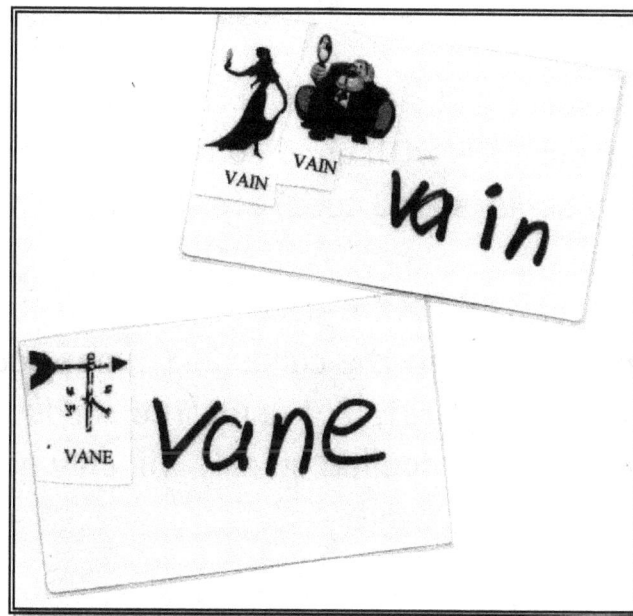

Break fast	**Snow** flake
Thorough	**Spr**ead

You can find the phonics rules by going to an internet search engine and typing in "phonics rules" or in a phonics book, available at libraries and bookstores.

Option 2:

Pre-test
Use pre-test errors to determine which letters should be in a **highlight color**.

Theory: Make the corrected mistake in spelling stand out so that the same mistake is not repeated.

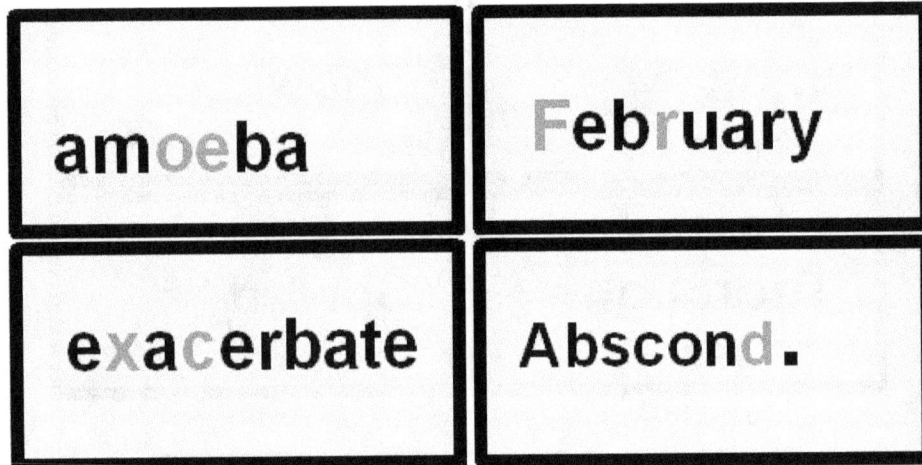

amoeba	February
exacerbate	Abscond.

1. Whenever possible, add clip art pictures to 'visualize' the word
2. Use bright color markers with good contrast to differentiate things
3. Add any other symbols, sound cues, etc. to make the spelling word more memorable
4. PRINT the words on INDEX CARDS
5. Practice by running through the cards 2-3 times each day for the four days before the spelling test. Put aside the cards that need more study. Cards that can be spelled quickly will only need to be reviewed on the first run.

Good luck! You should see a significant improvement in spelling test grades.

Three Card Match: Review Strategy

Materials

- Index Cards
  - Choose three of the following card colors: pink, green, blue, yellow or white
  - If you only have white cards or white paper, color-code the cards. For example:
    - Put a yellow dot or stripe on the word cards
    - Put a green dot or stripe on the picture cards
    - Put a pink dot or stripe on the definition cards...and so on and so forth
- Pictures
  - Of the item being reviewed
  - Related to the concept being reviewed
  - Mnemonic pictures to form an association

Instructions

1. Break down the information to be memorized into three related concepts, facts, pictures, meanings, etc.
2. Each card should contain one 'item' (see example below)

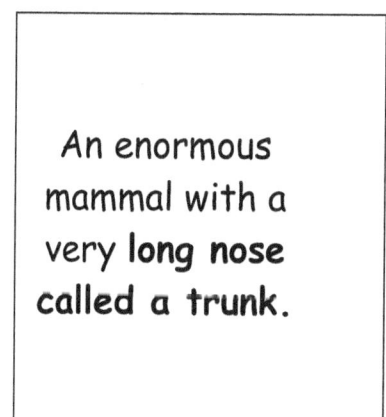

el·e·**ph**ant		An enormous mammal with a very **long nose** called a **trunk.**

3. Label the back of each card in a set with a number so that children can turn the card over and self-correct

For example:
> The word elephant, the picture of the elephant and the definition of the elephant would all be numbered #1 on the back.

> The word zebra, the picture of the zebra and the definition of the zebra would all be numbered #2, etc.

Hint: Children can make these sets from photocopied masters. See examples of sample masters on the next few pages. They are made with a word processor on the computer using the "table" function. Children simply cut and paste the items onto index cards.

Some children simply do not have legible handwriting. I recommend against forcing children to handwrite the cards unless they can print them clearly and legibly without taking an unreasonable amount of time to do so. Cards should be printed for greatest memory retention. Avoid cursive.

Options for use:

- Children can match the cards on their own as a review
- Children can pair up with a partner to match the cards

Research indicates that we learn the most when we teach others. When two people work together to study, they are teaching each other.

Matching Card Samples

Shape image	Formula	Name
 a a	a 2	square
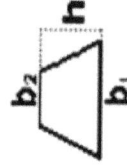 a b	ab	rectangle
 b h	bh	parallelogram
b_2 h b_1	h/2 (b1 + b2)	trapezoid
r (circle)	pi r 2	circle

Word	Visual	Definition
Folium of Descartes		$x^3 + y^3 == 3x*y$
Piriform		Parametric: {1,Sin[t]/h} * (1+Cos[t]). Period is 2 π.
el·e·**ph**ant		An enormous mammal with a very **long nose called a trunk.** They have curved tusks, huge, floppy ears and four long, thick legs.

Ze-bra		A large mammal with a **striped coat**, long legs and hooves. They are closely related to horses but have shorter manes.
Mam-mal		**Warm-blooded** animal with fur or hair on its skin and a skeleton inside its body.
cell		A tiny unit of plant or animal life, having a nucleus and surrounded by a very thin membrane.
mi-to-**ch**on-dria		Any of the very tiny **rod-like or string-like** structures that occur in nearly all cells of plants and animals and that process food for energy.

nu · cle · us		The part of a cell that **contains chromosomes**, which control growth and reproduction in most living things.
Pla-teau		A high, level area of land.
Val-ley		A long area of low land between mountains or hills. A stream or river often runs through a valley.
Word	**Visual**	**Definition**

"I don't know what to write!"

Clustering Activity

The clustering activity detailed on the following pages will help young children writing an essay or young adults filling out college applications.

Clustering Activity Step One

a. If your child has to write a paper, instruct him/her to draw a big circle on a piece of paper.

b. The topic of the paper should be put in the center of the circle. Note: If there is more than one topic, there can be more than one circle. For example, writing about three wishes would require three circles: one for each wish.

c. Instruct your child to write any thoughts, ideas or feelings about the topic in the circle. One can also ask questions about the topic or draw pictures of ideas.

d. Do not worry about spelling, grammar, sentences, etc. at this point. The purpose is to get the ideas out. Worry about writing rules later.

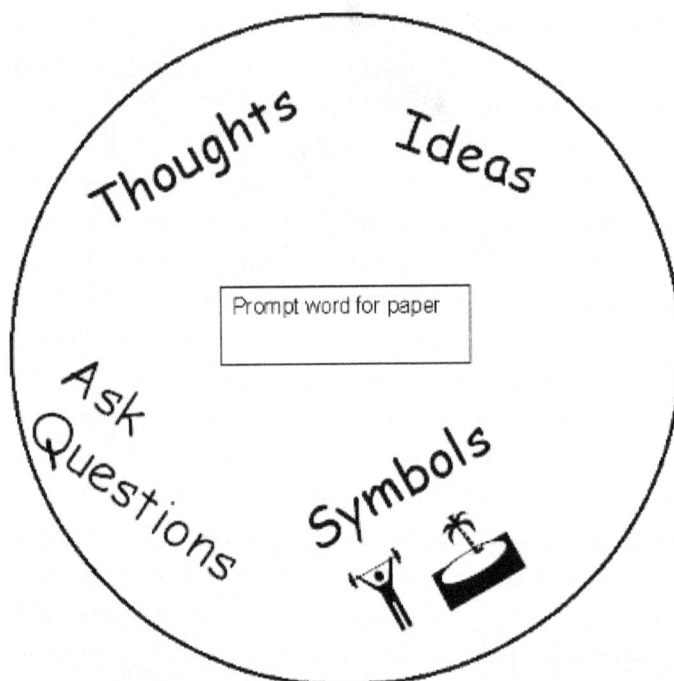

Thoughts Ideas

Prompt word for paper

Ask Questions Symbols

Make this circle BIG. At least the size of an 8" X 8" piece of paper.

e. After your child "creates" in the circle, allow him or her to share what he or she has written with you.

Clustering Step Two

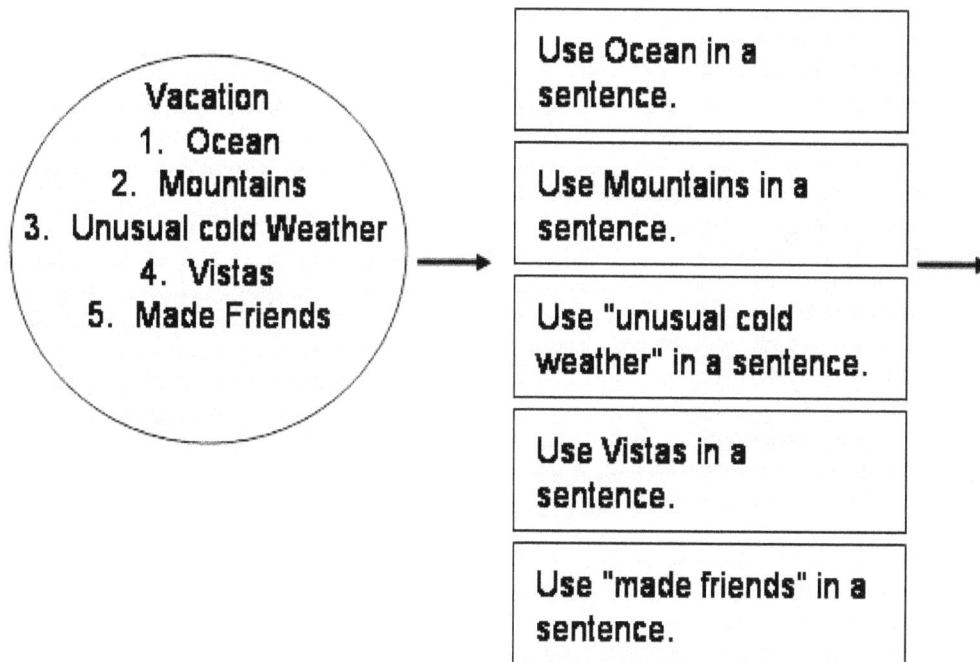

Vacation
1. Ocean
2. Mountains
3. Unusual cold Weather
4. Vistas
5. Made Friends

→

Use Ocean in a sentence.
Use Mountains in a sentence.
Use "unusual cold weather" in a sentence.
Use Vistas in a sentence.
Use "made friends" in a sentence.

→

a. Instruct your child to take the "best" words and ideas from inside his/her circle and use each word in a sentence.
b. These will be the topic sentences for the paragraphs he or she will write.
c. The sentences should be written on strips of lined notepaper or lined, sticky Post-It notes.

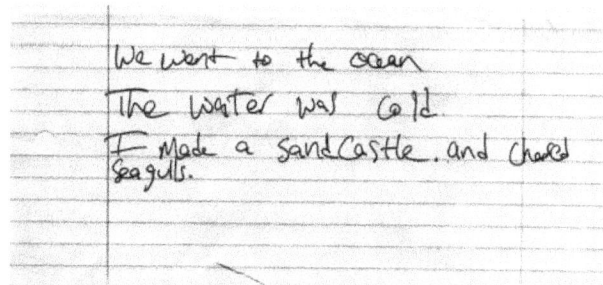

We went to the ocean
The water was cold
I made a sandcastle and chased
Seagulls.

Clustering Step Three

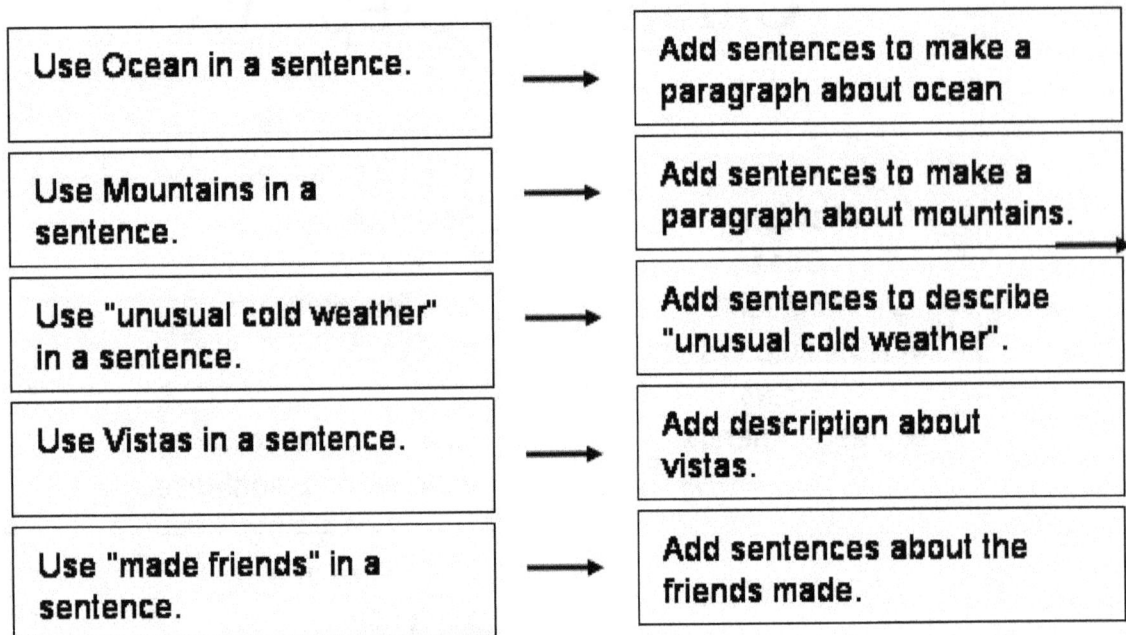

Use Ocean in a sentence.	→ Add sentences to make a paragraph about ocean
Use Mountains in a sentence.	→ Add sentences to make a paragraph about mountains.
Use "unusual cold weather" in a sentence.	→ Add sentences to describe "unusual cold weather".
Use Vistas in a sentence.	→ Add description about vistas.
Use "made friends" in a sentence.	→ Add sentences about the friends made.

a. Now, ask the child to take each sentence and add some more sentences about the topic sentence on the same strip of paper.

b. He or she should try to write two or three more sentences about the topic sentence.

*NOTE: Do not worry about spelling, grammar or punctuation at this point in the exercise. Worrying about the rules makes it more difficult to be creative.

Clustering Step Four

Add sentences to make a paragraph about ocean	**Add Introduction**
Add sentences to make a paragraph about mountains.	
Add sentences to describe "unusual cold weather".	Add
Add description about vistas.	
Add sentences about the friends made.	**Add Conclusion**

Next, have the child add an introduction and conclusion on separate strips of lined paper.

Clustering Step Five

Reorganize Paragraphs

Add Transitional Phrases

Introduction

Paragraph about the friends made.
Paragraph about mountains.
Description about vistas.
Paragraph about ocean
Paragraph describing "unusual cold weather".

Conclusion

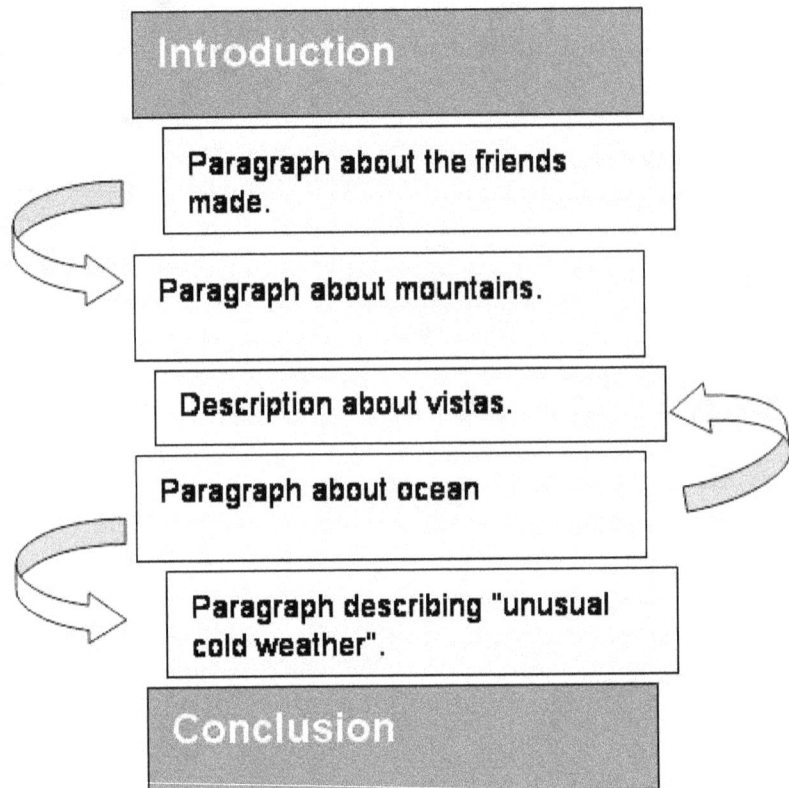

a. Next, have him or her move the strips of paper around so that the paper is in the best order and makes the most sense.
b. This process allows the writer to start anywhere in the paper. It frees up creative thought and encourages the process to start. Organizing the paper after the paragraphs are written is easy.
c. The strips should then be taped onto one or two big pieces of paper.
d. Ask the student to add transition words to make the paragraphs flow together.

Examples of Transition Words:

To Add:
And, again, and then, besides, equally important, finally, further, furthermore, nor, too, next, lastly, what's more, moreover, in addition, first (second, etc.);

To Compare:
Whereas, but, yet, on the other hand, however, nevertheless, on the other hand, on the contrary, by comparison, where, compared to, up against, balanced against, but, although, conversely, meanwhile, after all, in contrast, although this may be true;

To Prove:
Because, for, since, for the same reason, obviously, evidently, furthermore, moreover, besides, indeed, in fact, in addition, in any case, that is;

To Show Exception:
Yet, still, however, nevertheless, in spite of, despite, of course, once in a while, sometimes;

To Show Time:
Immediately, thereafter, soon, after a few hours, finally, then, later, previously, formerly, first (second, etc.), next, and then;

To Repeat:
In brief, as I have said, as I have noted, as has been noted;

To Emphasize:
Definitely, extremely, obviously, in fact, indeed, in any case, absolutely, positively, naturally, surprisingly, always, forever, perennially, eternally, never, emphatically, unquestionably, without a doubt, certainly, undeniably, without reservation;

To Show Sequence:
First, second, third (and so forth), A, B, C (and so forth), next, then, following this, at this time, now, at this point, after, afterward, subsequently, finally, consequently, previously, before this, simultaneously, concurrently, thus, therefore, hence, next, and then, soon;

To Give an Example:
For example, for instance, in this case, in another case, on this occasion, in this situation, take the case of, to demonstrate, to illustrate, as an illustration, to illustrate;

To Summarize or Conclude:
In brief, on the whole, summing up, to conclude, in conclusion, as I have shown, as I have said, hence, therefore, accordingly, thus, as a result, consequently, on the whole

Clustering Step Six

Rewrite or type into one continuous draft on full sheets of paper.

Hand in draft for teacher to correct.

Introduction
Paragraph about the friends made.
Paragraph about mountains.
Description about vistas.
Paragraph about ocean
Paragraph describing "unusual cold weather".
Conclusion

If the teacher is not correcting a draft, you may want to help your child with this step.

Clustering Step Seven

Student writes final draft incorporating teacher corrections, feedback and edits.

My Vacation
By Successful Student
Interesting new friends became the focal point of ….
The mountains were…
The vistas were inspiring as mountains met the ocean in a clash of green and aquamarine…
Unfortunately there was an unusual cold weather front….
Overall, the vacation was…

This is the point where the student will use the rules to make sure that spelling, grammar and punctuation are correct.

Method for Writing Better Sentences

Simple Sentence:

_____

Are there any words that can be made more specific?

_____

Who?	What?	When?	Where?	Why?

New improved sentence:
_____.

_____.

Is there another way this sentence could begin?

_____.

_____.

Math Writing Tip for Spatial Difficulties

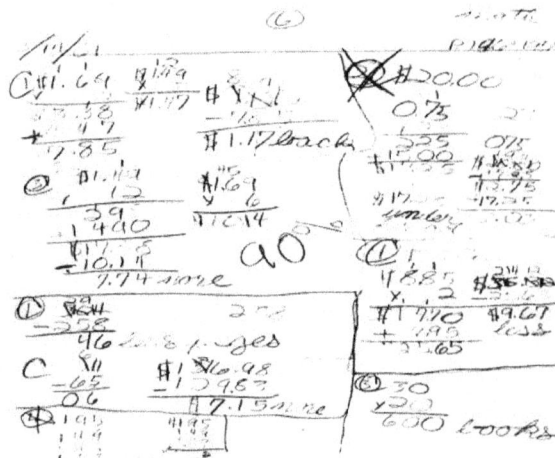

Are you tired of seeing math problems all jumbled up on an unlined piece of paper? Does it cause your child to make mistakes because numbers and equations are not lined up properly? Here is a simple solution!

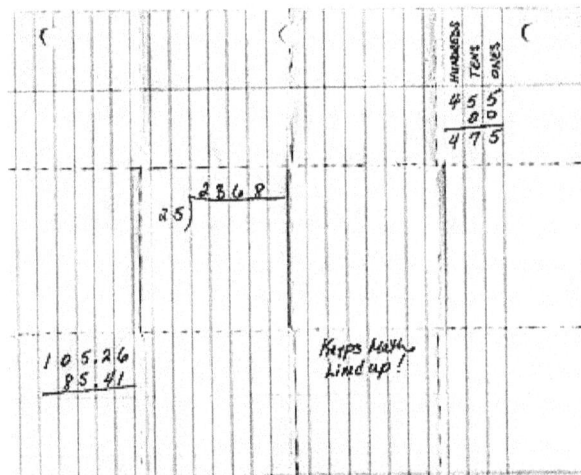

a. Keep math lined up!
b. Fold paper so that when you unfold it, it is sectioned into squares. See picture above.
c. Turn standard lined paper sideways.
d. Grid paper also works very well. You can make your own grid paper using the "Insert Table" function of your word processor.

Highlighting Activity

Put Prompts on Materials (or teach students to do it)

- ## Simple prompts on materials can help students succeed.

☆ Star at the starting point.

Arrow to indicate direction. ➡

START HERE ✓ Green mark to keep going

◉ **Bullets**

This is a strategy to teach children how to dissect and highlight an assignment so that they will "remember" all the parts.

When reviewing homework assignments with your child, use highlighters and color markers to dissect the information.

These prompts are presented in different colors. The simple act of picking up different colored highlighters or markers helps keep children involved and attentive.

Post-It Note Method of "Highlighting"

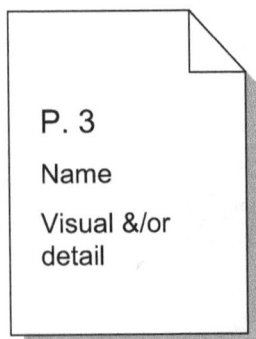

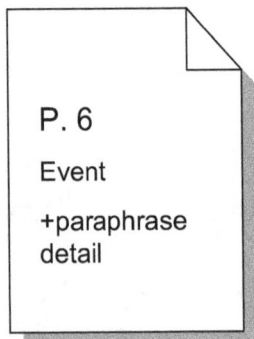

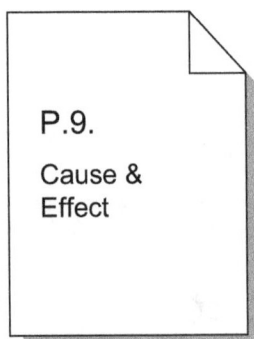

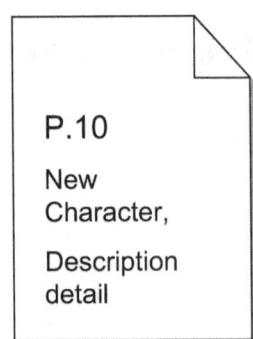

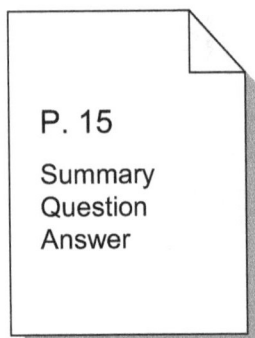

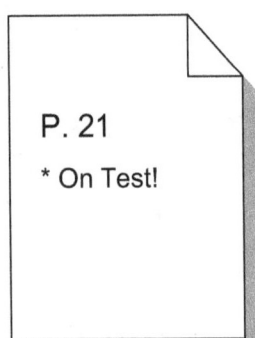

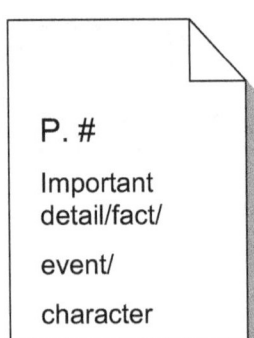

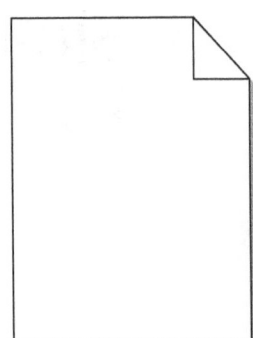

P. 3 Name Visual &/or detail	**P. 6** Event +paraphrase detail	**P.9.** Cause & Effect	**P.10** New Character, Description detail
P. 15 Summary Question Answer	**P. 21** * On Test!	**P. #** Important detail/fact/ event/ character	

As students are reading a text, every time an important fact, item, cause and effect situation, etc., comes up, have students put a post-it note right in that spot and write the page number, the item and a visual or some detail.

After the chapter is read, the novel is finished or the text section is done, children should take all the Post-it notes and line them up sequentially (as in the picture above) on a sheet of 8 ½ X 11 paper.

• Place the paper in a sleeve protector
• Children now have a study guide that is tied to the text

Draw It So You'll Know It

- Have your children draw pictures of what they are reading
- Have youth illustrate their notes with drawings that represent what is in the notes

This drawing was actually made using color markers. All of the pictures used in this handbook were originally done in color.

Sometimes current events are assigned and students must write about what they have read. For some learners, this is a very vague assignment that brings tears and the exclamation, "I don't know what to write!" Use the current event form in this section to help the student complete the assignment.

If the teacher has assigned a specific format for the way the current event report should look for his/her class, there are two options:

- Ask the teacher if he/she will accept this completed form instead
- Use this form as a way to structure the assignment and gather the information, then re-write it in the required format

Book Reports are often another source of frustration for students. Use the form on page 52 to gather the required information. There are prompts in the form that will help the young person understand what the different terms mean.

If the teacher has assigned a specific format for the way the book report should look for his/her class, there are two options:

- Ask the teacher if he/she will accept this completed form instead
- Use this form as a way to structure the assignment and gather the information, then re-write it in the required format

Current Event Form

Circle one: World   Nation   Local

Do this: Find a newspaper article that is interesting to you. Answer the following questions about the article. Attach the article or a photocopy.

Who is the story about? (Your answer could be a group of people, an organization or one person). _____

What event or happening does the article tell about?

_____

_____

_____

_____

Where did this event happen? (A city, a state, a building or an area)

_____

_____

When did the event reported on in the article take place? (Time, a specific day or date or a reference to a time: yesterday, last week, etc.)

_____

_____

Why did the event in the article happen? (Does your story explain what may have caused this to happen?)

_____

_____

What is your opinion about this article?

_____

_____

_____

Book Report

Title of Book:

_____

Author:

_____

Illustrator:

_____

Publishing Co.:

_____

Copyright date:

_____

Type of Story: (Mystery, historical fiction, science fiction, adventure, biography, etc.)

TIME:

    Historical period: (Medieval age, Victorian age, Early America, 1900's, etc.)

_____

    Duration: (Over what period of time does the story take place? One day, several weeks, one hundred years, etc.)

_____

PLACE:

    Geographical location:

_____

    Scenes: (Where does most of the story take place? Examples: outdoors, in someone's home, in a magician's castle, etc.)

_____

MAIN CHARACTER:

Name:

_____

Physical description: (What does he/she look like?)

_____

_____

_____

_____

Personality description: (What makes him/her special?)

_____

_____

_____

_____

How does this character change during the story?

_____

_____

_____

_____

What feelings does he/she go through?

_____

THE CONFLICTS IN THE STORY (The conflicts are the problems or hard decisions that the characters had to make)

_____

CONFLICTS/PROBLEMS	HOW DID YOUR CHARACTER DEAL WITH THE PROBLEMS?
1	

CONFLICTS/PROBLEMS	HOW DID YOUR CHARACTER DEAL WITH THE PROBLEMS?
2	

CONFLICTS/PROBLEMS	HOW DID YOUR CHARACTER DEAL WITH THE PROBLEMS?
3	

TELL SOME OF THE EXCITING THINGS THAT YOUR CHARACTER DID AND HOW HIS OR HER PERSONALITY MADE THESE PARTS EXCITING.

_____

_____

_____

YOUR OPINION OF THIS STORY:

What did you like about it?

_____

_____

_____

_____

What didn't you like about it?

_____

_____

_____

_____

Studies indicate that when students keep track of their grades, they go up. One step better: Have your child keep track of every grade on the Grade Review Sheet and then chart them in a bar graph.

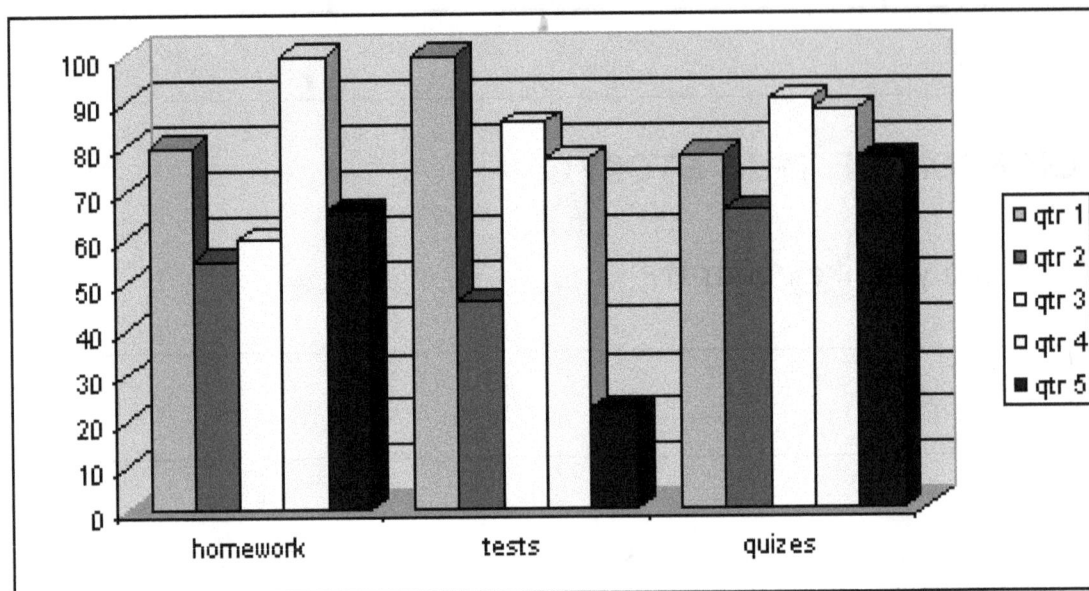

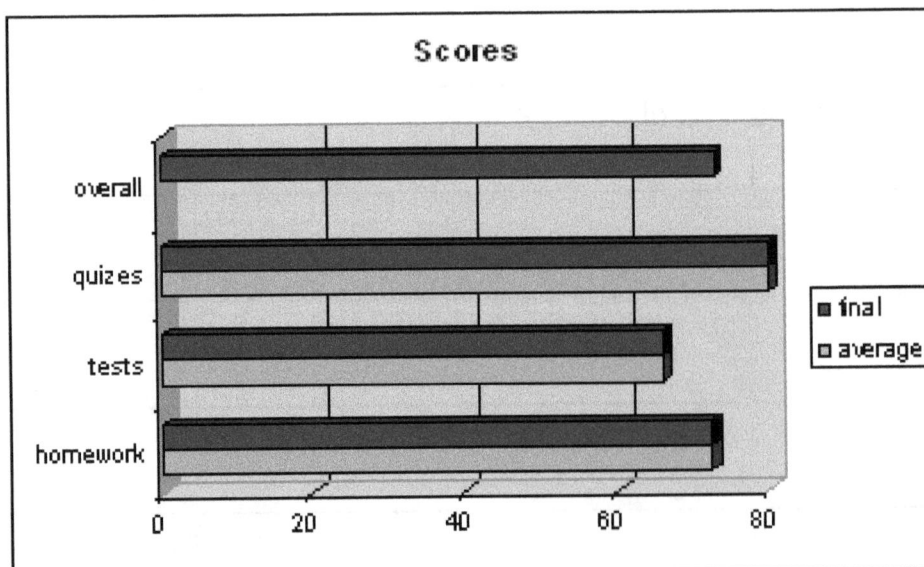

Team Name: _____   Quarter: _____

Grade Review Sheet

Name: _____   Class: _____

ASSIGNMENT TITLE, DATE, GRADE	HW %	CW %	QUIZZES %	TESTS %

- Include DATE, TITLE AND GRADE for each assignment received.
- This grade list should be kept in the front of your binder!
- Graph your grades so you can SEE how you are doing! Use a bar or line graph.

Writing Tool: Portable Text Editor

There are a few portable text editors currently on the market. Compare their capability, cost and adaptability to your situation. One example is the AlphaSmart 3000, a simple, portable and affordable computer companion. It is compatible with any computer, Macintosh or PC, and with most printers. It enables users to type, edit and electronically store text (for example, reports, essays, email messages or notes) and to practice keyboarding, without having to be at a computer. The text can then be transferred to any computer for formatting or sent directly to a printer. Its portability allows children to use it anywhere and anytime (for example, in the classroom, at home or on field trips). The AlphaSmart has an optional 100% error-free IR (infrared) interface that allows wireless transfer between the AlphaSmart and a computer or printer.

Mandalas as a Tool to Focus, Calm and Get Creative

Mandala: a geometric or pictorial design usually enclosed in a circle

- Working from the center to the edge: Broadens attention
- Working from the edge to center: Focuses attention
- Relaxes the body
- Activates the Right Brain
- Visual Prompt/structural map for writing down feelings in a poem, song or composition
- "Tilt the brain so language comes out differently" – Caryn Mirriam-Goldberg, author of "Write Where you are" Free Spirit Press

A source for mandalas can be found at http://www.mandali.com/

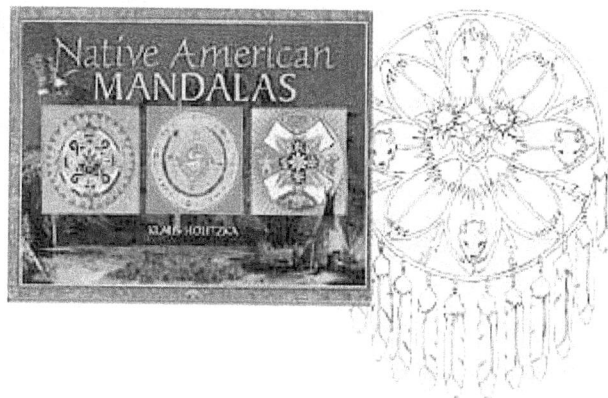

Offer Mandalas to your child if he/she is stressed, having difficulty with a writing assignment or simply needs to calm down and get ready to work.

Color Your Own Mandala

- Sample from Monique Mandali , *Everyone's Mandala Coloring Book*, *http://www.mandali.com/*

Problem Solving Mind Map

Imagine that a young person comes to you with a problem and asks for your help to solve it. The problem-solving form on the next page gives you a structure in which to discuss the problem.

For example, John comes home and complains that Chris is picking on him. He wants to beat Chris up.

- Take out the form and lay out the problem
- In the top section write: Chris is picking on me

- **Go to the first column. Where it says possible solution write:**
- Beat Chris up
- Do not make a value judgment
- List the pros/benefits of beating Chris up
- List the cons/disadvantages (negative consequences) of beating Chris up

- **Consider another solution:** Talking things out with Chris
- Go to the second column. Where it says possible solution write:
- Talk it out
- Do not make a value judgment
- List the pros/benefits of talking it out
- List the cons/disadvantages (negative consequences) of talking it out

- **Continue brainstorming other options and follow the same process.**

Now, John can be encouraged to make the best choice for him: one that has the most benefits and the fewest negative consequences.

This process can be used to make many types of decisions or to solve many different kinds of problems.

PROBLEM

POSSIBLE SOLUTION

ADVANTAGES

DISADVANTAGES

POSSIBLE SOLUTION

ADVANTAGES

DISADVANTAGES

POSSIBLE SOLUTION

ADVANTAGES

DISADVANTAGES

Organizing All That School Paperwork

Landmark Notebook System Materials List

The Landmark Notebook System is designed to help you keep your papers, assignments, handouts, etc. organized and in a location where you can find them when you need to refer to them again. Like any new system, it requires practice and discipline until it becomes a habit.

You will need:

- [ ] One 2" binder. You can put two subjects in one binder. (Four subjects require two binders)
- [ ] Portable three-hole punch
- [ ] Zippered pouch with holes to fit in the binder
- [ ] A ruler with 3 holes
- [ ] 8-section dividers for binders
- [ ] Two three-hole divider pockets
- [ ] Two highlighters of different colors
- [ ] Post-it notes
- [ ] Small Package of skinny colored markers or gel pens
- [ ] Highlighter tape
- [ ] Pens and pencils
- [ ] Three hole reinforcers
- [ ] One accordion file for each subject in a binder
- [ ] Assignment calendar/notebook

Set up your binder this way:

Work from the front and put the pieces in the following order:

- Three-hole punch
- Ruler
- Zippered pouch with highlighters, writing utensils, tape, reinforcers, etc.
- Assignment calendar
- Divider labeled HOMEWORK
- Divider labeled NOTES
- Divider Labeled TESTS/QUIZZES
- Divider Labeled HANDOUTS
- Pocket Divider
- Dividers for the second subject, labeled the same way

1. Use the sections for homework, notes, tests/quizzes and handouts for one lesson or chapter/unit.

2. When the unit is finished, move ALL the papers to your accordion file for that subject and label that section with the unit name.

3. Save the accordion file at home for midterms and final exams. Do not throw study materials away!

For more information, contact Landmark Foundation @ 508-927-4440, www.landmarkschool.org

Add Checkboxes:

Draw checkboxes next to each step of an assignment to help your child remember to complete all of the steps. Check them off once they are done.

Example below:

NAME_____PER_____DATE_____

CONSTELLATION PROJECT CHECKLIST

CHECK OFF EACH ITEM AS YOU COMPLETE IT!

☐ **Look up the constellation in a book (there are books in the library and the science class)**

☐ **Draw the pattern of the stars that make it up**

> A. Use plain white paper
> B. Use BLACK ink or pencil
> C. Make it no LARGER than 3 ½ " (height) X 8" (length)

☐ Connect the star patterns with DASHED lines

☐ Cut out your constellations and mount them on BLACK construction paper at the TOP of the sheet

☐ Pierce PIN HOLES (not massive holes) through the stars

☐ Look up the myth about your constellation

☐ Write the story (myth) in YOUR OWN WORDS

☐ The final draft should be in PEN on plain WHITE PAPER

☐ State where the myth comes from

☐ Mount the myth BELOW your constellation on the black construction paper (8 ½" X 11")

Use Microsoft Word Readability Statistics to Improve Writing

If students know what the readability level of their writing is, they can challenge themselves to bring it up higher! All they have to do is use words with more syllables and write longer sentences that are more complex and then spell check again to see if their reading level is higher!

To display readability statistics in MSWord (These instructions are for MSWord 2000):

- On the *Tools* menu, click *Options* and then click the *Spelling & Grammar* tab
- Select the *Check grammar with spelling* check box
- Select the *Show readability statistics check box* and then click *OK*
- Click *Spelling and Grammar* on the Standard toolbar
- When Word finishes checking spelling and grammar, it displays information about the reading level of the document

TIP:
When copying and pasting text from Internet web sites into Microsoft Word:

1. *Edit/Copy* then highlight text from the website
2. Go to your MSWord document
3. Click on *Edit* then choose *PASTE SPECIAL*
4. Paste as Formatted or Unformatted text, NOT HTML

Now you can work with the information without the interference of invisible web code.

Acknowledgment
Dr. Mary S. Neumann, DHAP, NCHSTP, "Developing Effective Educational Print Materials"

To view the readability of a document in Word Perfect:
1   Click *Tools Grammatik*
2   Click *Options Analysis Readability*
3   In the Readability dialog box, choose a comparison document from the Comparison document list box

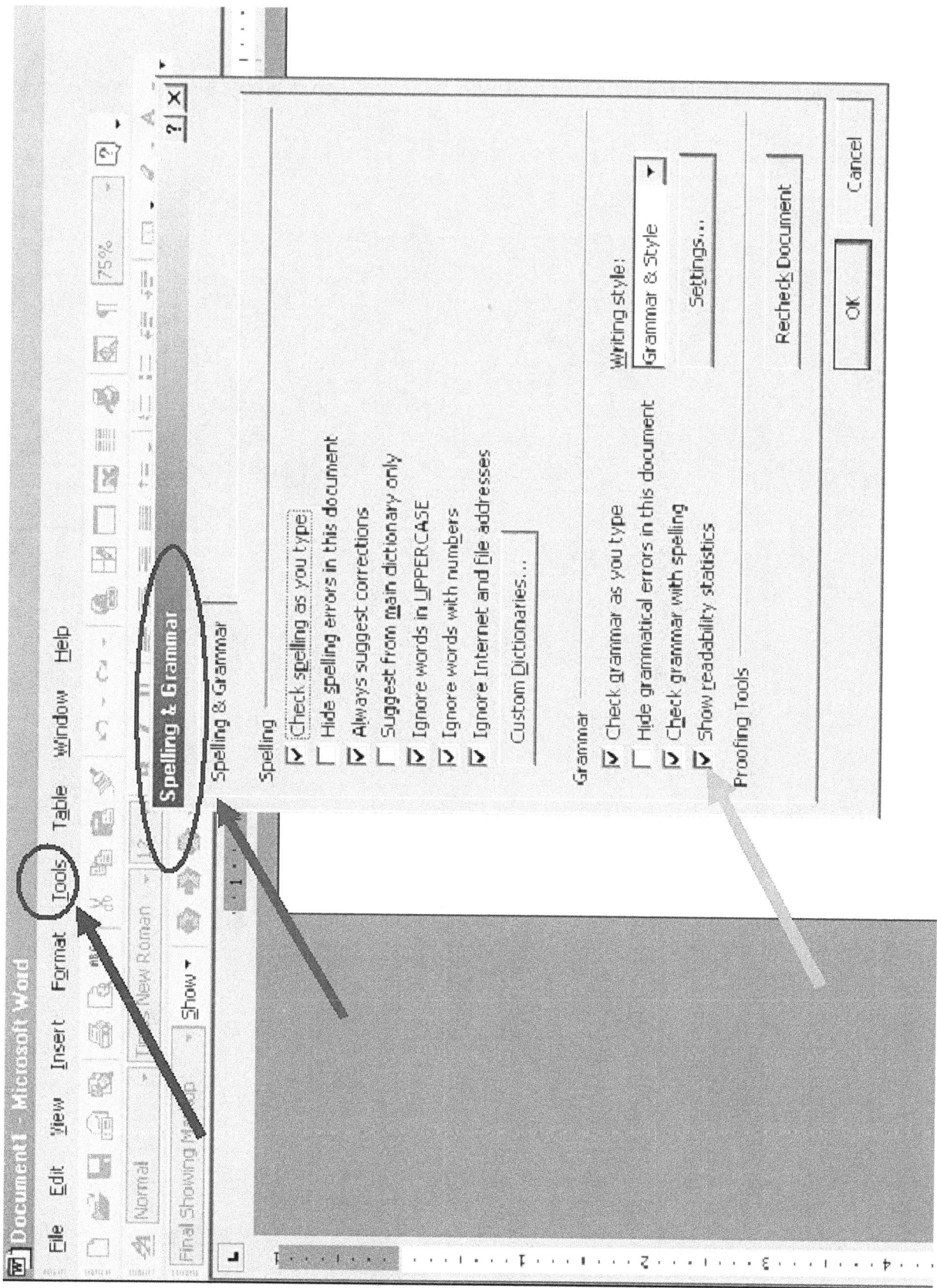

AutoSummarize in MSWord

Use AutoSummarize to highlight key points or to create an abstract or summary of your writing.

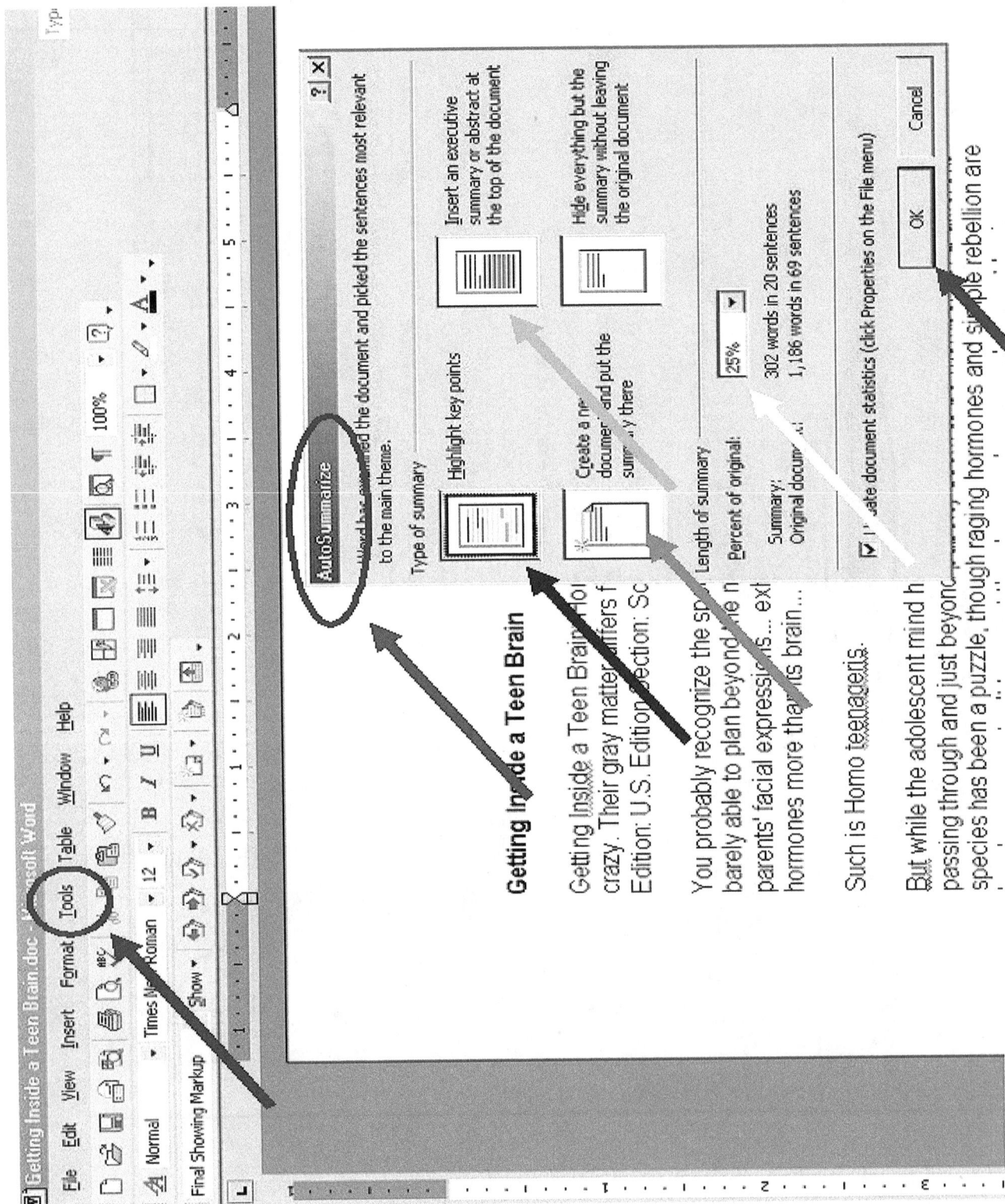

APPENDIX - RESOURCE LISTS

Books and Resource Articles

BEHAVIOR MANAGEMENT
Fitzell, Susan

- <u>Free The Children: Conflict Education for Strong Peaceful Minds,</u> New Society Publishers, 1997

Glasser, William, MD

- <u>Control Theory,</u> New York: Harper & Row, Inc., 1984
- <u>Reality Therapy,</u> New York: Harper & Row, Inc., 1975
- <u>Schools Without Failure,</u> New York: Harper & Row, Inc., 1975

Good, E. Perry

- <u>In Pursuit of Happiness: Knowing What You Want, Getting What You Need</u>, New View Publications, 1987

BRAIN BASED LEARNING
Caine, Geoffrey, & Caine, Renate Nummela & Crowell, Sam.

- <u>Mindshifts: A brain-based process for restructuring schools and renewing education.</u> Tucson, AZ: Zephyr Press. 1994
- <u>Making connections: Teaching and the human brain.,</u> Alexandria, VA: Association for Supervision and Curriculum Development. 1991

Jensen, Eric

- <u>Brain-Based Learning,</u> Turning Point Publishing, 1996
- <u>Brain Compatible Strategies,</u> Turning Point Publishing, 1997
- <u>Teaching with the Brain in Mind</u>, ASCD, 1998
- <u>The Great Memory Book</u>, The Brain Store, 1999

Greenleaf, Dr. Robert K

- <u>Brain Based Teaching: Building Excitement for Learning, 2000 Edition complete with applications</u>
- <u>The Power of Two</u>
- <u>The Question,</u>
    - ➤ To order Call 401-782-8507

Sylvester, Robert

- <u>A Celebration of Neurons: An Educators Guide to the Human Brain</u>, ASCD, 1995

COOPERATIVE LEARNING
Putnam, JoAnne W

- <u>Cooperative Learning and Strategies for Inclusion: Celebrating Diversity in the Classroom</u>, Paul H. Brookes,

---

COOPERATIVE LEARNING

1993 ISBN 1-55766-134-0

BRAIN COMPATIBLE APPROACH

Lewis, Barbara

- The Kids Guide to Social Action, Free Spirit Press, 1991

DiSpezio, Michael

- Critical Thinking Puzzles, Sterling Publishers, ISBN 0-8069-9430-4 (Mnemonics)

LEARNING DISABILITIES

Bell, Nancy and Lindamood, Phyllis

- Vanilla Vocabulary, Academy of Reading Publications, 1993

Heacox, Diane

- Up From Underachievement, Free Spirit Press, 1991

Rief, Sandra and Heimburge, Julie

- How To Reach & Teach All Students In The Inclusive Classroom. The Center for Applied Research, 1996

Sedita, Joan

- Landmark Study Skills Guide Landmark Foundation, Call (508) 927-4440 Ext. 2116, www.landmark.pvt.k12.ma.us/landmark

Schumm, Jeanne Shay and Yddencich, Marguerite

- School Power, Free Spirit Press, 1992 (This book is a gold mine for providing photo-copyable forms for students to organize writing and reports.)

Tomlinson Carol Ann

- The Differentiated Classroom ISBN: 0-87120-342-1

Winebrenner, Susan

- Teaching Kids with Learning Difficulties in the Regular Classroom: Strategies and Techniques Every Teacher Can Use To Challenge & Motivate Struggling Students, Free Spirit Publishing, 1996

Friend, Marilyn and Bursuck, William D.

- Including Students with Special Needs: A Practical Guide for Classroom Teachers, 3/e, Publisher: Allyn & Bacon, Copyright: 2002Format: Paper, 544 pp ISBN: 0-205-33192-0

MULTIPLE INTELLIGENCES

Armstrong, Thomas

- Multiple Intelligences In The Classroom, ASCD, 1994

Armstrong, Thomas

- Multiple Intelligences In The Classroom, Association for Supervision & Curriculum Development; ISBN: 0871203766; 2nd edition (May 15, 2000)

Gardner, Howard.

- Frames of mind: The Theory of Multiple Intelligences. (Paperback ed.). Basic Books, 1985

MULTIPLE INTELLIGENCES

- The Unschooled Mind: How Children Think and How Schools Should Teach. Basic Books, 1991

Gibbs, Jeanne
- Tribes: A New Way of Learning and Being Together, Center Source, 1987

Lazear, David
- Seven Ways of Teaching, Skylight Publishing, Inc., 1991

PEER TUTORING

Ashley, W., J. Jones, G. Zahniser, and L. Inks.
- Peer Tutoring: A Guide To Program Design. Research and Development Series No. 260. Columbus: Ohio State University Center for Research in Vocational Education, 1986. ED 268 372.

Bloom, B.
- "The Search for Methods of Group Instruction as Effective One-to-One Tutoring." EDUCATIONAL LEADERSHIP 41 (1984): 4-17.

Cohen, P.
- "Outcomes of Tutoring." AMERICAN EDUCATIONAL RESEARCH JOURNAL 19 (1982): 237-248.

Crushon, I.
- Peer Tutoring: A Strategy For Building On Cultural Strengths. Documentation and Technical Assistance In Urban Schools, 1977. ED 228 367.

PERSONALITY TYPES

Lawrence, Gordon
- People Types & Tiger Stripes, CAPT, Inc. 1996

Silver, Strong and Perini
- So Each May Learn: Integrating Learning Styles and Multiple Intelligences, ASCD. 2000

TEST BIAS & GRADING

Berk, R.A. (Ed.).
- "Handbook of methods for detecting test bias." Baltimore, MD: The Johns Hopkins Univ.Press.1982

Estrin, Elise Trumbull

Alternative Assessment: Issues in Language, Culture, and Equity, 1993
http://www.eric.ed.gov/ERICDocs/data/ericdocs2sql/content_storage_01/0000019b/80/16/1f/ae.pdf

Munk, Dennis & Bursuck, William
- Report Card Grading Adaptations for Students with Disabilities: Types and Acceptability, Intervention in School & Clinic, 1 May 1998

Munk, Bursuck, & Olson
- The Fairness of Report Card Grading Adaptations: What Do Students With and Without Learning

Disabilities Think? Remedial & Special Education, 1 Mar 1999.

Produced by the ASPIIRE and ILIAD IDEA Partnerships in cooperation with the U.S. Department of Education.

- Making Assessment Accommodations: A Toolkit for Educators, Video captioned in English and Spanish. 2000, 146 pages. 14 minutes. ISBN 0-86586-3644, Council For Exceptional Children, #P5376 $99.00/CEC Members $69.00

VISUAL ORGANIZERS

Buzan, Tony

- The Mind Map[6] Book. ISBN 0 563 86373 8, 1993.

Booher, Dianna.

- Clean Up Your Act; Effective Ways to Organize Paperwork and Get It Out of Your Life

Haber, Ralph N

- "How We Remember What We See". Scientific America, 105, May 1970.

Margulies, Nancy

- Mapping Inner Space: Learning and Teaching Mind Mapping

Rico Lusser, Gabriele

- Writing The Natural Way ISBN: 0-87477-186-2 and 0-87477-236-s (ppbk.)

---

[6] "Mind Map" is a registered trademark of the Buzan Organization 1990.

Catalogues for Recorded Book Loans, Rentals and Sales

Audio books combine important ingredients for creating a successful lifelong reader.
Audio books:

- Motivate students to read
- Allow students to enjoy a book at their interest level that might be above their reading level
- Allow slower readers to participate in class activities
- Provide a way to learn the patterns of language, learn expressions and increase vocabulary
- Are good examples of fluent reading for children, young adults and for people learning English as a second language
- Build the neural connections necessary for auditory processing skills, which are required for literacy
- Improve listening skills
- For pre-reading, they familiarize students with the story so that they can concentrate on the words when they read the text
- Bring a book to life thereby inspiring, entertaining and linking language and listening to the reading experience
- Build a reading scaffold--broadening vocabularies, stretching attention spans and flexing thinking skills

1. Recorded Book Rentals (800) 638-1304 Telephone
2. Books on Tape (800) 626-3333 Telephone
3. Chivers Audio Books (800) 621-0182 Telephone
4. Blackstone Audiobooks (800) 729-2665 Telephone
5. The Teaching Company (800) 832-2412 Telephone (Sells taped lectures on history, literature, etc. Ask to hear their free sample lecture on "How to Understand and Listen to Great Music," one of a series of 16 lectures on music.)
6. Recording for the Blind & Dyslexic (800) 221-4792 Telephone (They have 75,000 unabridged books on tape. They also sell portable four-track cassette players from $99 to $199. Students can get textbooks custom-recorded; ask for information. Fees are $50.00 to apply and $25.00 per year thereafter—all the books you can read; no postage required. Application form includes a form for your doctor to sign.)

World Wide Web Resources

The links below are also available online at
http://www.aimhieducational.com/inclusion_urls.html

Website URL	Topic	Category
http://www.aimhieducational.com/inclusion.html	29 Positive Aspects of ADD/ADHD	ADD
http://www.sensorycomfort.com/	Resources for ADD, Autism	Autism
http://www.explosivechild.com	The Explosive Child	Behavior
http://www.explosivechild.com	Helping easily frustrated, inflexible children	Behavior
http://www.judyringer.com	Making More Powerful Choices	Behavior
http://www.ldonline.org/ld_indepth/teaching_techniques/strategy_cards.html	Using Strategy Cards to Enhance Cooperative Learning for Students with Learning Disabilities	Behavior
http://www.wglasser.com/	William Glasser Institute	Behavior
http://www.aimhieducational.com/books/spedbooks.html	Brain Gym Resources	Brain
http://www.aimhieducational.com/inclusion.html	Brain Research Sheds New Light on Student Learning, Teaching Strategies, and Disabilities	Brain
http://brainconnection.positscience.com	Brain Based Learning site	Brain
http://www.brains.org/hottopics.htm	Hot Topics in Current Research	Brain
http://powerof2.org	Collaboration	Collab
http://www.marilynfriend.com	Co-teaching, collaboration and grading	Collab
http://www.powerof2.org/	Resource site for collaborative teaching	Collab
http://www.aimhieducational.com/inclusion.html	Imagine Teaching Robin Williams- Twice-Exceptional Children in Your School	Diversity
http://www.aimhieducational.com/inclusion.html	10 Resource Articles: Bilingual, ESL, Multicultural	Diversity
http://www.ginnyhoover.com/learning.htm	Learning Style Resource	Diversity
http://www.hots.org/	Poverty and Learning	Diversity
http://www.myersbriggs.org/applying/education.cfm	Using MBTI Type in Education	Diversity
http://www.nldline.com/	Non-Verbal Learning Disorder	Diversity
http://www.pbs.org/wgbh/misunderstoodminds/	Misunderstood Minds	Diversity
http://www.weaverclinic.com/	Learning Style and attention issues	Diversity
http://www.hes-inc.com/hes.cgi/02120.html	The Teacher's Resource Guide (A strategy goldmine)	Ed Gen
http://www.teachersplanet.com/special.shtml	Teacher Resource	Ed Gen
http://www.teachervision.com	General Resource	Ed Gen
http://www.teachnology.com/	The Web Portal for Educators	Ed Gen
http://www.csun.edu/~vcecn006/	Writing Resource	English
http://www.neo-direct.com/intro.aspx	AlphaSmart Text Editor	Equip

Website URL	Topic	Category
http://www.dryerase.com/	High Quality Dry Erase Boards	Equip
http://www.fullspectrumsolutions.com/index.html	Source for Full Spectrum Lighting	Equip
http://www.keyboardinstructor.com	Text Editor & Applications	Equip
http://www.stokespublishing.com	Teach Timer	Equip
http://www.hardin.k12.ky.us/res_techn/sbjarea/math/JeopardyDirections.htm	Jeopardy Game Directions	Game
http://www.cec.sped.org/bk/catalog2/assessment.html	Assessment Tool Kit	Grading
http://www.fairtest.org/index.htm	National Center for Fair & Open Testing	Grading
http://www.help4teachers.com/	Layered Curriculum	How-to
http://www.humboldt.edu/~lfr1/kindling.html	Lesson Plan: Kindling - Making it Meaningful	How-to
http://www.aimhieducational.com/books/spedbooks.html	Books on Topics covered in seminar	Inclusion
http://www.aimhieducational.com/books/spedbooks.html	Paraprofessional's Guide to the Inclusive Classroom	Inclusion
http://www.inclusion.com/	Inclusion Resource	Inclusion
http://www.ualberta.ca/~jpdasddc/INDEX.html	Inclusion Resource	Inclusion
http://www.wrightslaw.com/	Special Ed Law Advocates	Law
http://tmwmedia.com/algebra_tutor.html	Algebra Tutor Video	Math
http://www.aimhieducational.com/books/spedbooks.html	Visual Math: See How Math Makes Sense	Math
http://www.aimhieducational.com/inclusion.html	Graphic Organizers	Math
http://www.dotolearn.com	Math grids and much more	Math
http://www.fasenet.org/store/kay_toliver/eddiefiles.html	Math Videos	Math
http://www.marcycookmath.com	Zip Around Cards, I have/Who has?	Math
http://www.mathgen.com/remedial.htm	Math Resource	Math
http://www.rogertaylor.com/	Click on Resource Library for Math Songs	Math
http://www.teachingideas.co.uk/maths/contents.htm	Math Ideas	Math
http://www.tsbvi.edu/math/index.htm	Teaching Math to visually impaired students	Math
http://www.aimhieducational.com/inclusion.html	Reading, Writing, Rapping	Music
http://www.jazzdigger.com/b/Ron_Brown/	Music to Teach by	Music
http://www.musicintheclassroom.com/	Music to Teach by	Music
http://www.neilslade.com	Music to Teach by	Music
http://www.rocknlearn.com/	Learning to Music	Music
http://www.shakeandlearn.com	Grammar, math, science and language to music	Music
http://www.songsforteaching.com/index.html	Music to Teach by	Music
http://www.homeworknow.com	Online homework resource	Org
http://www.landmarkschool.org/	Binder & Study Skills	Org
http://www.blackvoices.com/	Maya Angelou	Other
http://www.lucidcafe.com/library/currentread/currentread04.html	Nikola Tesla	Other
http://educationnorthwest.org/	List of Model Programs	Program

Website URL	Topic	Category
http://www.scientificlearning.com/	Fast ForWord;Develops language & listening skills for reading.	Reading
http://www.sundancepub.com/c/@5RKYpnKw1bYvA/Pages/index.html	Reading Resource	Reading
http://school.discovery.com/schrockguide/assess.html	Rubrics	Rubrics
http://www.rubrics4teachers.com/	Rubrics	Rubrics
http://school.discovery.com	Science Resource	Science
http://www.ericfacility.net/ericdigests/ed433185.html	Science Classrooms for Students with Special Needs	Science
http://www.webelements.com/	Interactive Periodic Table	Science
http://www.readplease.com/	Reads any web page, makes mp3/wav files, zooms any page, text-only version web pages, translates and much more!	Software
http://www.computerautomation.com/	Special Education Automation Software	Software
http://www.inspiration.com/	Graphic Organizer Software	Software
http://www.brainchild.com	Online assessments of state tests	Software & Tech
http://www.mimio.com	Interactive whiteboard technology	Software & Tech
http://www.disabilityresources.org/FAMOUS.html	Famous people with LD	SpEd
http://www.disabilityresources.org/index.html	Resource	SpEd
http://www.iser.com/	LD Professional Directory	SpEd
http://www.ldonline.org/	LD Online Resource	SpEd
http://www.lrpdartnell.com/cgi-bin/SoftCart.exe/scstore/01_Special_Ed/cat-IDEA.html?E+scstore	Special Education Products	SpEd
http://muskingum.edu/~cal/database/	Learning Strategies Database	strategy
http://www.aimhieducational.com/inclusion.html	Cut and Paste 101	strategy
http://education.umn.edu/NCEO/AccomStudies.htm	Online Accommodations bibliography	Tools
http://puzzlemaker.school.discovery.com/	Puzzlemaker	Tools
http://us.dk.com/?11CS^home	Dorling Kindersley	Tools
http://wikkistix.com	Hands on Learning, Figit Toys	Tools
http://www.aimhieducational.com/books/spedbooks.html	Mandala Coloring Books	Tools
http://www.aimhieducational.com/brainchild.html	Brainchild: Technology builds English & Math Mechanics in line with State Standards	Tools
http://www.epraise.com	Recognition Products & ideas	Tools
http://www.graphicorganizers.com/	Graphic Organizers- many free samples	Tools
http://www.mindbinders.com/	Mindbinders Study Cards (Those cute ones on a ring)	Tools
http://www.schoolhousetech.com/	Worksheet Factory	Tools
http://www.studygs.net/	Study guides and strategies	Tools
http://www.sunburstmedia.com/	For Language Learners	Tools
http://www.teachervision.fen.com/lesson-plans/lesson-6293.html	Graphic Organizers	Tools
http://www.thinkingmaps.com/	Visual Teaching Tools	Tools

Website URL	Topic	Category
http://www.trainerswarehouse.com	Teacher & Presenter Supplies	Tools
http://www.mindtools.com/memory.html	Tools for improving Memory	Tools
http://vischeck.com	See what it's like to be color blind	Visual
http://www.oepf.org/	Behavioral Optometry	Visual
http://www.pavevision.org	Parents Active for Vision Education	Visual
http://www.tsbvi.edu	Blind and Visually Impaired	Visual
http://www.vis-ed.com/	Visual Ed Study Card Sets	Visual
http://www.drawingwriting.com/index.html	Drawing/Writing and the new literacy	Writing
http://www.stepuptowriting.com/default.asp	Multi-sensory writing strategies	Writing

Safe School

Caring Community

WORKSHOPS FOR PARENTS, PARENT EDUCATORS AND TEACHERS

Susan has successfully completed 21 hours of Parent Learning Network Parent Educator Training sponsored by the Texas Association of School Boards. She is trained to deliver workshops based on the *Family Frameworks* and *The Early Years* curricula. The curricula was written by the Texas Association of School Boards staff members in cooperation with content researchers across Texas.

The curricula units emphasize active learning techniques that empower participants to become their own problem solvers. The lesson plans offer activities that appeal to the multiple intelligences and promote learning the way the brain is best and biologically designed to learn. Participants will have an opportunity to share ideas, support each other, study current research, and work together as a team to find answers to their questions.

Workshop Topics

- Choices and Consequences: Bullying
- Finding Balance in Stressful Lives
- Parents & Schools Working Together
- Peer Pressure
- Please Help Me With My Homework!
- Understanding Yourself and Others: Keys to Better Relationships
- Why Won't Children Listen?

Program costs:
Costs are determined on an individual basis.

Contact information:
To schedule a consultation/ training or for more information, telephone 210-473-2863 from 7:00 a.m. EST through 8:00 p.m, EST, Monday through Friday . Fax: 210-473-2863.
E-mail: sfitzell@aimhieducational.com* www.aimhieducational.com

Cogent Catalyst Publications

an AIMHI Educational Programs partner company

Customer information

Name: _____
Street: _____
City, State & Zip: _____
Phone 1: _____
Phone 2: _____
Email Address: _____

Order Date: _____

Shipping & Handling

Order Total	Shipping Price
Up to $55.00 (except P	Free Shipping
Large posters (< 10)	$7.95
$55.01 - $70.00	$9.95
$70.01 - $100.00	$11.95
$100.01 - 149.00	$13.95
More than $149.01	10% of Subtotal

All orders are shipped via USPS and can be expected within 14 days of the time we receive your order. Items ordered at one time are shipped together whenever possible.

Qty.	Description	Unit Price	Discounted/Bulk Price	Line Total
	Co-Teaching and Collaboration in the General Classroom 2nd Ed.	$24.97		
	Set of 10: Co-Teaching and Collaboration		$199.97	
	Free the Children: Conflict Education for Strong, Peaceful Minds	$15.95		
	Set of 10: Free the Children		$124.97	
	Paraprofessionals and Teachers Working Together 2nd Edition	$24.97		
	Set of 10: Paraprofessionals and Teachers		$199.97	
	Please Help Me With My Homework: English 2nd Edition	$10.97		
	Set of 10: Please Help Me		$87.97	
	Please Help Me With My Homework: Spanish	$10.97		
	Set of 10: Please Help Me		$87.97	
	Special Needs in the General Classroom 2nd Edition	$24.97		
	Set of 10: Special Needs		$199.97	
	Transforming Anger to Personal Power	$23.95		
	Set of 10: Transforming Anger		$199.97	
	Umm Studying? What's That?	$15.00		
	Set of 10: Umm Studying?		$119.97	
	Memorization & Test Taking Strategies DVD Training Program	$895.00		
	Flash Cards: Special Needs in the General Classroom	$7.95		
	Flash Cards: Umm Studying... What's That?	$7.95		
	Poster- MOODZ: Laminated 8 1/2" x 11"	$4.95		
	Poster-MOODZ: Gloss Coverstock 18" x 24"	$9.95		
	Poster-Feed The Future One Drop at a Time 15" X 11" (standard size)	$9.95		
	Poster Set-Response to Intervention	$29.95		
	Resource CD: Ready-Made Forms & Tools 2010	$9.95		
	Sticky Notes "Best Ideas"	$2.50		
	Write-In:			
	Write-In:			
	Write-In:			

****Large posters require shipping because of tube mailers

Subtotal:	
Shipping & Handling:	
Total:	

The portion below must be filled out or your order will not be processed

☐Cash   ☐Check   ☐Visa/MC

Visa/MC#_____   Exp.Date: _____

Make checks payable to Susan Fitzell